JOURNEY TO A STRAW BALE HOUSE

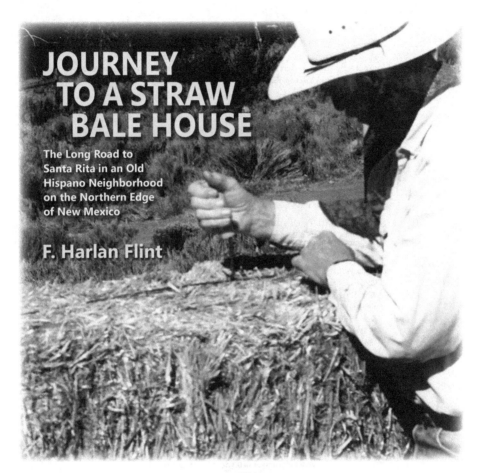

JOURNEY TO A STRAW BALE HOUSE

The Long Road to
Santa Rita in an Old
Hispano Neighborhood
on the Northern Edge
of New Mexico

F. Harlan Flint

Sunstone Press

SANTA FE

Sunstone books may be purchased for educational, business, or sales promotional use.
For information please write: Special Markets Department, Sunstone Press,
P.O. Box 2321, Santa Fe, New Mexico 87504-2321.
Photographs by Chris Flint
Body typeface › IPoliphilus MT Pro
Printed on acid-free paper
∞
eBook 978-1-61139-462-7

———————————————————————————————————————

Library of Congress Cataloging-in-Publication Data

Names: Flint, F. Harlan, 1930-
Title: Journey to a straw bale house : the long road to Santa Rita in an old
  Hispano neighborhood on the northern edge of New Mexico / by F. Harlan
  Flint.
Description: Santa Fe : Sunstone Press, 2016.
Identifiers: LCCN 2016005384 (print) | LCCN 2016009378 (ebook) | ISBN
  9781632931207 (softcover : alkaline paper) | ISBN 9781611394627
Subjects: LCSH: Flint, F. Harlan, 1930---Homes and haunts--New Mexico--Santa
  Rita. | Flint, F. Harlan, 1930---Travel. | Flint, F. Harlan,
  1930---Family. | Santa Rita (N.M.)--Biography. | Straw bale houses--Design
  and construction--New Mexico--Santa Rita. | Santa Rita (N.M.)--Buildings,
  structures, etc.
Classification: LCC F804.S33 F55 2016 (print) | LCC F804.S33 (ebook) | DDC
  978.9/692--dc23
LC record available at http://lccn.loc.gov/2016005384

———————————————————————————————————————

SUNSTONE PRESS IS COMMITTED TO MINIMIZING OUR ENVIRONMENTAL IMPACT ON THE PLANET. THE PAPER USED IN THIS BOOK IS FROM RESPONSIBLY MANAGED FORESTS. OUR PRINTER HAS RECEIVED CHAIN OF CUSTODY (COC) CERTIFICATION FROM: THE FOREST STEWARDSHIP COUNCIL™ (FSC®), PROGRAMME FOR THE ENDORSEMENT OF FOREST CERTIFICATION™ (PEFC™), AND THE SUSTAINABLE FORESTRY INITIATIVE® (SFI®). THE FSC® COUNCIL IS A NON-PROFIT ORGANIZATION, PROMOTING THE ENVIRONMENTALLY APPROPRIATE, SOCIALLY BENEFICIAL AND ECONOMICALLY VIABLE MANAGEMENT OF THE WORLD'S FORESTS. FSC® CERTIFICATION IS RECOGNIZED INTERNATIONALLY AS A RIGOROUS ENVIRONMENTAL AND SOCIAL STANDARD FOR RESPONSIBLE FOREST MANAGEMENT.

———————————————————————————————————————

WWW.SUNSTONEPRESS.COM
SUNSTONE PRESS / POST OFFICE BOX 2321 / SANTA FE, NM 87504-2321 /USA
(505) 988-4418 / ORDERS ONLY (800) 243-5644 / FAX (505) 988-1025

For Christine M. Flint and Baudelio Garcia,
my Partners and Teachers

Contents

Prologue

This is in part a story about building a house. It is also about a lifetime leading up to that project. But as you will see this was not a regular, ordinary, run of the mill house. It is special for many reasons, one being that it was to be a handmade house, built by my family and me and a couple of friends with the help of a few other people who had the skills to do the things we were unable to do for ourselves.

A handmade house. That's the only kind of house that people have lived in for most of human history, and that goes back a way. Wikipedia, my source for anthropological knowledge, reports that humans, Homo sapiens, "reached anatomical modernity about 200,000 years ago and began to exhibit behavioral modernity about 50,000 years ago." We were slow learners. Even in the most recent millennium, when we were well along the learning curve towards behavioral modernity, building one's own house was still the norm in most of the world. Suddenly in the last few centuries that ceased to be the case and today it is extremely rare, at least in the so called developed world, so we approached this most elemental of human tasks with a sense of how special it was.

I know I started out calling it a house but it was really a cabin. A cabin is not a full time, permanent dwelling. It is even more meaningful because it is a place to get away to, even if one doesn't have anything in particular to get away from. In our case it was a dream, a preoccupation for many years before it became a reality. It was the product of imagining and planning that occupied many leisurely afternoons and quiet winter evenings. But I'm getting ahead of myself. There's much to be said about how we came to that endeavor before we begin to describe the project itself.

Like many stories this one involves a place, a narrative and a cast of characters. The place is a special piece of land along a river in a remote, isolated valley on the edge of the wilderness at the northern border of New Mexico. The chain of events starts with the meandering journey that brought us first to New Mexico and much later to the place where we would ultimately build our cabin The cast of characters includes the people encountered along the way whose lives touched ours and influenced our course through life, some of whom helped us in the 1995 adventure of building a handmade cabin in the New Mexico wilderness. As is often the case in life, the final destination was no more important than the journey.

It is perhaps surprising that a person with my beginnings should come to have a lifelong passion and enthusiasm for things Spanish in general and New Mexican in particular. Born in Rhode Island, I spent my early years in New England, on the Atlantic coast. What place could be more remote geographically and culturally from Spain and New Mexico? For starters, the difference in scale of the two states is shocking. Rhode Island is only thirty seven miles wide and forty eight miles tall and contains only 1,055 square miles. New Mexico's Rio Arriba County, the locale of much of our story, is 5,846 square miles in size and could contain almost six Rhode Islands. Ethnically, historically and culturally the two states could hardly be more different. When I was young, Rhode Island was a culturally diverse state in its own way but with a far different cultural and racial mix than that of New Mexico. Its population was drawn primarily from Europe, its people ranging from the United Kingdom originating Yankees to all shades of northern and southern Europeans. I guess the Yankees were at the top of the pecking order but there were many Scandinavians, Germans and other northern Europeans. Southern Europe was well represented by Portuguese, Italians and even some Greeks, but almost no Spanish. It had a religious mix of Catholics, Protestants and Jews and a smattering of other creeds. The Native Americans who had originally lived there had almost completely disappeared, leaving only their names on many places including the state's dominant inland salt water feature, Narragansett Bay. There were also a significant number of African Americans in the state. One additional piece of Rhode Island's ethnic mix deserves to be mentioned. The French Canadians shared the northern New England frontier with my grandfather and great grandfather who were Maine Yankees. Both of these peoples lived along the frontier between the United States and Canada at the same time the New Mexico *Hispano*s were venturing into northern New Mexico and southern Colorado to share that frontier with the new people who were then arriving from eastern America. Many French Canadians, regionally called Canucks, migrated south from northern New England and were well represented in Rhode Island's population.

As a child I was unaware of any significant racial divide in Rhode Island. There seemed to be few African Americans or Asians in our communities, but ethnicity and religion were factors we were aware of at an early age and served as a proxy for race when it came to social, economic and cultural ranking. Religious and ethnic prejudices were evident in the lives of children, even those among of us who lived in relatively homogeneous suburban communities. My parents taught us the basics of tolerance and equality but we were well aware of the stereotypical norms of our predominantly northern European and Protestant traditions. We were often confused about the fine points of ethnic and religious intolerance and not clear on how to distinguish between darker complexioned Italian Catholics and lighter skinned but mysteriously alien Jews. I remember that some of my playmates demonstrated this ambiguity by referring to neighboring "others" as "Wop Jews," a mixed media error that grew out of local versions of ignorance and insensitivity. In terms of religion, my own family was on the extreme left fringe of the Judeo-Christian tradition. We were more or less Unitarians. We were taught to be tolerant of all manner of unusual beliefs and to constantly challenge our own. Religion and ethnicity as sources of conflict are ubiquitous in the history of this country and, indeed, in the history of the world. My first consciousness of this phenomenon happened to occur in Rhode Island but it would reappear and have impact throughout my life journey to a destination in northern New Mexico, many years later.

So how does a young person from such a background develop a sense of intimacy and affection for things Spanish? Perhaps, with apologies, it could be called a quixotic quest. Sorry. It started, of all unlikely places, in Vermont where I was a student at the Putney School for my first two years of high school. It was my remarkable good fortune there to be introduced to the Spanish language and culture by an amazing teacher, Mara Moser. She had been a Spanish citizen and spoke a pure Castilian version of the language. As her name may suggest, she was of Jewish heritage and had suffered from the latest version of the cyclical persecution of Jews that has marred the history of Spain. She fled from the regime of *Generalísimo*

Francisco Franco during the Spanish Civil War and somehow found her way to a small, progressive private boarding school on a farm in Vermont.

I was a haphazard and uninspiring student but the force of her personality and her ability to teach the language and its cultural context left an indelible mark. She had a way of bringing the language to life even for restless adolescents. I vividly remember that she offered idiomatic alternatives to the Spanish word for the devil, *el diablo*. To this day, whenever I hear a reference to the devil I think of him as *Su Majestad Infernal*, His Infernal Majesty. Thus began my lifelong journey.

After two years at Putney I returned to Rhode Island and a small public high school that didn't offer third and fourth year Spanish so I was tutored for my last two high school years, a program that offered few conversational opportunities. I was given the gift of two months in Spain in the summer of 1948, the year of my graduation, an experience that opened my eyes, my mind and my imagination. The program was a Georgetown University sponsored "*Curso de Verano Para Norteamericanos*" at the University of Madrid. The old university had been destroyed by the Civil War and the new campus was surrounded by desolate destruction. It was on the western edge of Madrid, isolated from the main city, and was surrounded by war ruins and a barrio of shacks occupied by citizens who had been uprooted by the war. I later observed that Madrid's topography had a remarkable resemblance to Albuquerque's, at least to the eye of an impressionable teenager.

I was the youngest participant in the program and most of the others were teachers and professors or at least card carrying adults. But there was one other young guy, a Cornell University junior by the name of Rodrigo de Llano from Laredo, Texas. On our first night at the University he adopted me and led us off into the barrio of tar paper shacks where we were enthusiastically welcomed by the locals who exuberantly shared their wine with us until the wee hours. Rodrigo taught me conversational Spanish with a Mexican lilt, how to meet the real people of Madrid, how to drink wine from a *bota* (Spanish wine bag), and many other things that have served me well over the years.

One class-skipping afternoon in the quiet of a 100 degree day we had an experience that brought home the meaning of irony. We were headed downtown for some frivolous purpose, probably to go to a wine bar, when to our surprise we came upon two men digging a ditch in the heat of the day while all other workers were out of sight, enjoying their siesta. Rodrigo asked them why they were the only ones there. The older worker, a veteran of the Republican Civil War Army, said he had to do extra work so he could feed his wife and children. The younger guy said he had to do extra time so he could afford to marry his sweetheart.

My Mexican American friend introduced me to his version of Spanish language and culture which were very different from my introduction to old Spain and Castilian Spanish by Mara Moser. At summer's end I was as close to fluent in the language as I would ever be. Two years at Swarthmore College in Pennsylvania gave me exposure to a more academic perspective and an introduction to Spanish literature, reading Spanish novels, including the monumental *Don Quijote*, but it did little to sustain my fragile conversational skills. To a degree, the same was true of my next two years at the University of New Mexico in Albuquerque. New Mexico introduced me to my third Hispanic culture, that of the unique, New Mexico-based *Hispano* people, the descendants of the first settlers of Nuevo Mexico, who lived there in their isolated, homogenous Spanish speaking community for about two hundred and fifty years until the Americans arrived in the middle of the nineteenth century.

My introduction to New Mexico could best be described as an accident of family history. It was a result of my father's rampant wanderlust. In the best of times he could be described as impractical, certainly eccentric and maybe a little bit crazy in a benign sort of way. He had long been restless in his unsatisfying law practice in Providence and in 1950 his exotic tendencies took a fairly dramatic turn. Things came to a head when

I was a sophomore at Swarthmore College. He and my mother had sent my two younger brothers to the Putney School in Vermont for the school year. The absence of three sons gave my father the logistical flexibility he needed for what came next. Throwing caution to the wind, he resigned from the firm of Adler, Flint and Zucker, put the house on the market, put all their worldly goods in storage and he and my mother and my two younger sisters hopped in the car and set out on a grand tour that had no identified end point.

They left Rhode Island in January, headed on a generally westward trajectory, pausing along the way at historic sites, national parks and monuments and other attractions and ended up, by chance, in Albuquerque in the middle of March with the spring winds blowing a gale and the dust storms billowing. At the age of fifty four he was having a midlife adventure on steroids, and steroids hadn't even been invented yet. He was obviously having the time of his life. The day after their arrival he went out and bought a house. I say "he" because my mother was far too practical and down to earth to have participated in such a hare brained scheme. He then began to address the question of how he could make a living in his new home town. That question was answered quickly as he found employment in a dominant industry of this post war boom town. He would be a real estate agent.

I watched this cryptically reported madness with amazement and a bit of admiration from the relative peace and quiet of my suburban Philadelphia campus. It soon became apparent that the straightened financial circumstances of our new life style would make the cost of my private eastern college hard to manage. That and the lure of New Mexico helped me decide to follow the family west to Albuquerque and the University of New Mexico. So it was that my New Mexico life began, more by chance than by choice.

Despite my bizarre introduction to New Mexico, it lived up to my expectations and then some. The place overwhelmed me: the space, the distances, the mountains, the sharp, dry landscape and the little Hispanic villages and Indian pueblos. The Sandia Mountains towering over Albuquerque reminded me of the mountains of Madrid that I experienced just two years before. The panoramic long range views were a complete departure from the short sight lines of my earlier New England life. But above all it was the people and the sound of spoken Spanish around me every day that inoculated me once again with my teenage romance with things Spanish.

I loved the place from the first day but I was grieving over the distance between me and a girl on the other side of the continent. We sustained our long range relationship for a while, with the help of a summer spent with her and her family in Princeton, New Jersey, but at the age of about twenty one I couldn't for the life of me see how it could work in the long term and as is usually the case in these affairs, it didn't and we tried to move on. I struggled with my sense of loss and was at best a perfunctory student at the university. At the end of the spring semester of 1952, I was floundering as a student and decided that my life needed a kick start and a sharp change of direction. By that time my father had suffered a recurrence of his wandering syndrome and he and the family had pulled up stakes in New Mexico and for no visible reason had headed off for Portland, Oregon. My own odyssey took me to the United States Army Recruiting Office and I joined up. But in the meantime I had become a committed New Mexican. It had been a brief two year stay for me but I had my green card and could claim New Mexico as my home. During my stay I had found some chances to practice my Spanish but it wasn't enough to perfect my transformation. Despite my best efforts I was destined be an Anglo.

My army time exposed me to another Hispanic culture. Many of my fellow recruits in basic training at Fort Ord, California were Puerto Rican draftees, so Spanish and Spanglish were part of daily life. The nearby town of Monterrey had been part of Spanish and Mexican territory, though evidence of that history was slim in the 1950s, but there were many Spanish speaking locals in the area. I continued to try my tentative

Spanish whenever there was a chance. I remember going into a shabby Army bar in the vicinity of the base while enjoying one of my weekend passes. I must have been there before and had tried to impress the locals with my basic Spanish because when the waitress saw me she said to the bar tender, "Hey Joe, it's the red headed Mexican!"

At Fort Benning, Georgia, where I attended the Infantry Officer Candidate School in 1953, my so called cubical mate was Clark Font, the only Puerto Rican in our class. Through the magic of alphabetical roommate assignments, he and I became great friends and I was exposed to Spanish with a Puerto Rican accent. I was probably headed for Korea but on the eve of our completion of training the armistice was declared. After graduating and becoming a Second Lieutenant, I was assigned as a platoon leader in a basic training company at Fort Lewis, Washington. Almost all the young soldiers in my platoon were Puerto Rican draftees who spoke little English. My company commander was a battle hardened veteran who had fought bloody battles in Korea, leading his mostly Puerto Rican troops who he affectionately called "mis tigres."

After leaving the army I returned to Albuquerque and the University of New Mexico. As a twenty five year old veteran I was seen to be mature enough to be hired as the student manager of the Student Union Building, the center of social life at the University. I lived in the building and it was a big part of my life in that first year back. Among the regulars for coffee and lunch were members of the language faculty including Rubén Cobos and Sabine Ulibarri who became my friends and teachers.

A new way of life began in 1955, just a week or two after I returned to New Mexico, when I met Chris Mason, an Indiana native, just arrived in New Mexico and a new teacher in the Albuquerque public schools. Chris was a recent graduate of Indiana University where she had majored in Spanish. We met in the Triangle Bar, a student hangout on the edge of the University campus. She and her sister, who I had known during my earlier University tour, had retreated to the Triangle to take the edge off their first Parent-Teacher meeting. After an animated conversation Chris drove me home to the Student Union building. One thing led to another, as things do, and she's been taking me home ever since.

But the story can't be cut that short. She was a cute, feisty girl with beautiful dark brown hair, a strong personality and a sense of humor that have delighted me and her ever expanding family ever since. She had spent her first year of teaching in Frankfort, Indiana after graduation from Indiana University and had just escaped a drab small town life to take a chance in the west. We were immediately comfortable with each other and I fell for her hook, line and sinker. Sorry for the dated terminology. She and her sister shared a rental house with another young teacher and we spent quite a bit of time there since neither of us had the discretionary income to support more exotic entertainment. The other girls were very thoughtful and frequently retired to their rooms to give us privacy. One evening after a couple of beers, (it's always a couple, isn't it?), we returned to the house and had a long conversation. We had only known each other for about two months and had a lot of ground to cover. It was so relaxing on the couch and we were so reluctant to call it a day that I dozed off. When I more or less returned to my senses, I said with little premeditation, "Will you marry me?" I was immediately wide awake when she instantly answered, "When?" I knew then that she was not a woman to be trifled with and responded forcefully and convincingly, "Gosh, I don't know. I haven't really thought about it." But we did soon think about it and were married in her parents' living room the following June after her father and grandfather made a quick trip to New Mexico to check me out and reported to her mother that "he doesn't seem to have any glaring faults." After all that drama and with that glowing endorsement ringing in my ears, we launched out on our honeymoon drive back to Albuquerque. In three hard but thrilling years, Chris and the G.I. Bill put me through law school, in the course of which we welcomed our wonderful first child, Christine Elizabeth, better known as Tina.

During one law school summer I worked as a laborer doing road maintenance work in the hot city streets of Albuquerque. All of my co-workers were New Mexico Hispanics who were disbelieving when they learned that in one year I would be a lawyer, *un abogado*. One guy summed it up by saying, "If I had your education I wouldn't do anything but walk around all day writing things down in a little book." He obviously had an eye for the basic requirements of management. Spanglish was our common language and I learned useful phrases such as "*Esta tiempo para lonche*" (It's time for lunch) and "*Dame una mache*" (Give me a match). Another good law school experience was working as a volunteer in the downtown Legal Aid office where many of our clients were *Hispano* people dealing with the legal problems of people living close to or below the poverty line, a common condition in New Mexico.

After graduation and a move to Santa Fe with our new daughter, we found ourselves living in a community that still had a majority *Hispano* population. Despite cultural and linguistic differences, Santa Fe was a place where people came together across the divide in their working lives and in their residential neighborhoods. My colleagues in the Attorney General's office and the State Engineer's office were a good mix of *Hispano*s and Anglos.

My *Hispano* friendships and my growing attraction to the people, their culture and communities didn't happen without a bump or two in the road. One was a little more significant than the others. One of my colleagues in the Attorney General's office was one of the first *Hispano*s to graduate from the new law school at the University of New Mexico.

There were many *Hispano* lawyers in New Mexico but in most cases they had all gone to law school elsewhere, often at Georgetown University in Washington while they were working for a Congressman or a Senator or in some government office that provided them with income that gave them a chance to pursue a legal education. I had many conversations with my colleague about his years growing up in the small village of Truchas. It was at an elevation of 9,000 feet, high up on the slopes of the Truchas Peaks north of Santa Fe. Almost all of its inhabitants were *Hispano*s. Among the few flat landers in the village were a handful of Presbyterian missionaries and teachers who came to enlighten and convert the Catholic citizens of the village. His tales of the extended and often interrelated families of the community were intriguing and beguiling to me, in part because they were so different from my own family stories. The children of the community moved seamlessly from one household to another. If they were present at meal time it was accepted that they would share the host family's meal as if they were meant to be there. It sounded like the perfect example of the village raising the child.

When my new friend left state employment to launch his private law practice, we began to discuss the possibility of my joining him. Most of the prominent law firms in Santa Fe were comprised almost exclusively of Anglo lawyers and most of the more successful *Hispano* lawyers were working for state and local government or were in elective office. The decade of the 1960s was a period of civil rights activism and I was inspired or deluded to think that a partnership with Antonio would be a small contribution to that effort. Many of my Anglo friends and co-workers warned me against the move, primarily on economic grounds. My wife was also rightly worried about giving up my modest but secure salary for the uncertainty of a startup private practice. Despite these concerns but with Chris's blessings, I decided to take the plunge.

It was a disaster. A lawyer friend in another state office referred a live client who provided the only fees I earned in my short adventure in the private sector. It turned out that the romance of Antonio's stories failed to put food on our table. Chris supplemented my nonexistent financial contribution by working as a substitute teacher, paying half of her meager hourly wage to her sister in law for babysitting our small children. We were clearly in deep trouble. My partner wasn't bringing in clients or legal fees and it became clear that his charismatic charm and unquestioned skills were offset by his lack of discipline and a weakness for alcohol.

With sadness, regret and embarrassment I asked my friend, the Attorney General, if he would take me back. He quickly agreed, without recrimination, and I retreated to the Attorney General's office with my tail between my legs. No one second guessed my ill-considered adventure and I was soon happily writing briefs and arguing cases before the New Mexico Supreme Court. I soon left to become General Counsel for the State Engineer and Interstate Stream Commission and had a satisfying tour as the state's head water lawyer.

Looking back on it, I have no regrets about my leap of faith and modest act of conscience. In addition to learning how hard it was to start a law practice, I gained perspective on how much more difficult it was for a young Hispanic lawyer to make his way as a professional minority in a majority Anglo environment. Things are better today, in part because the University of New Mexico is a national model for enrolling, supporting and graduating *Hispano*s, Native Americans, women and other minority students. The law school's clinical law program teaches not only the law but also the mechanics of the business of lawyering.

There is no doubt that I entered into that vocational excursion with an abundance of naiveté but the outcome did not cause me to be cynical or pessimistic about the possibility for positive change in the world and I've continued to occasionally support losing causes. One lesson learned was that while *Hispano*s were willing and anxious to enjoy the benefits of the majority American society, they didn't want to abandon the attributes of their culture and heritage that they continued to value. It may be presumptuous but it seems to me that they didn't want to assimilate in the manner of immigrant minorities in eastern America. New Mexico *Hispano*s were here first. They were not the immigrants and that gave them even more reason to preserve what they could of their ancient culture, language and way of life.

Chris and I had bought our first little house in a new development on the south side of town but regretted that we were not living in the heart of the old town. Two years later we were able to buy an adobe house at the upper end of the Santa Fe River canyon in a neighborhood that had been a Hispanic enclave for generations. The area had only recently become popular with Anglo newcomers like us. Some of the new people loved the physical beauty and ambiance of old Santa Fe but were uncomfortable sending their children to the local elementary school where the overwhelming majority of the students were from *Hispano* families. It had been common practice for Anglo parents to have their children transferred to "better" schools where their children would not be in the minority. Chris and I felt that if we were to live in that neighborhood our children should go to the neighborhood school and what a good decision that proved to be.

For a variety of reasons including the disempowering demographics of our neighborhood, our local school had been disadvantaged in the competition for scarce resources. Despite the city's substantial if not majority *Hispano* population, the Santa Fe School Board had long been dominated by the more aggressive Anglo political figures. We and our neighbors, working together through a revitalized Parent Teacher Association, mobilized to bring about change and increase support for our school. The process was its own reward. We made new friends and gained a real sense of community. Pot luck dinners were organized in the school cafeteria and occasionally in our homes and these activities brought an ever expanding number of parents into our campaign. Most of the children were from families where Spanish was spoken in their homes and our gatherings were lively and bilingual. Our own three children had the good experience of learning what it was like to be part of the ethnic minority in a public space. Large delegations of parents attended school board meetings and made their voices heard with considerable impact and things began to change.

On a personal level our connection with our new neighbors was a revelation for us. We began to learn more about the history and traditions of our *Hispano* friends. We found that their reliance on Spanish as their language at home was not seen as a disability or handicap. Rather it seemed to be a necessary if not indispensable part of keeping their cultural traditions alive. Throughout our time in the company of *Hispano* people, the importance of culture was frequently emphasized. Preservation of all elements of their traditions was a high priority of parents. Inherited art forms were handed down from mother and father to sons and daughters. The sense of family was strong, a condition that was becoming less common among the more mobile and uprooted Anglo families. The *Hispano* families were almost always Catholic and the annual rhythms of the church calendar and its associated rituals were pervasive and nurtured by the role of the beautiful Cristo Rey church, an important symbol of community in our neighborhood.

Vicky and Nabór Lucero exemplified these patterns of life. They passed on the traditional skills of wood carving and two of their sons had become celebrated Santeros when we later returned to Santa Fe after a twenty year hiatus. Vicky herself was displaying her traditional colcha embroidery at Santa Fe's annual Spanish Market. In the years of our school based collaboration Nabór often entertained us with his guitar and he and Vicky sang Spanish folk songs that were part of their family traditions. Vicky and other *Hispano* ladies often provided New Mexico cuisine at school events that contributed to the fun and enthusiasm of our group.

Our school based collaboration led me to run for the Santa Fe School Board. In my first race I was targeted in a Spanish language editorial as a gringo outsider. I was competing against a well-known and respected *Hispano* dentist and we were contesting for much of the same constituency; people who felt the board was not dealing with the concerns of the more disadvantaged students. That meant that I was vying for the same *Hispano* voters with whom he had an obvious advantage. The race was close but I lost. A few months later another board member announced he would not seek reelection. My former adversary contacted me and said, "We would like you to run and you will have our support." That collective "we" meant that the informal but influential *Hispano* political network would be made available to me. With that help and influence and with the support of my neighbors, the same editorial writer who had originally opposed me now enthusiastically touted my qualifications, in Spanish, and I won the election. We and our neighbors and supporters celebrated and I worked with my new colleague and other board members to push for the reforms and attitude changes we believed would allow greater academic success for all students.

Chris and I and our three children marinated in the warm and nurturing atmosphere of Santa Fe and our neighborhood during those early Santa Fe years. In 1970, my family and I made the difficult decision to move away from New Mexico to pursue greater financial security, a common New Mexico thing to do. For the next twenty years we were expatriates, living in Alaska, California, Ohio and Utah. Even as we all wandered off to distant places for a while, the experience of those years left an indelible imprint on our consciousness and we still treasure the memories of that time these several decades later. In the mean time we were back often and our strong ties to New Mexico were reinforced by our participation in the 1977 purchase of the Rio de Los Pinos property that would be the site of our building adventure.

That circuitous narrative may help to explain the intense emotional and psychological pull that was the foundation of our love of New Mexico and ultimately led to the experience of building a house in a place that was so connected to its *Hispano* history. And descendants of the *Hispano* settlers, in a little place that we learned was called Santa Rita, were to be important contributors to our project.

Early Days

As sketched out above, I had returned to New Mexico in 1955 after my Army time and the state was our home until 1970 when our family ventured off on a typical nomadic American career that, except for visits, took us away for twenty years. We went first to Alaska, a far different place from New Mexico in almost every way. It's true that the Spanish navy visited and made claims on it during colonial days but they had little lasting impact. They left only a few place names like Cordova and Valdez (now pronounced Val Deez). During our first year there I had a long distance conversation with an old political acquaintance, Ernestine Durán Evans, who had just completed a term as New Mexico Secretary of State. For reasons I have never understood she had decided that she wanted to move to Anchorage and open a New Mexico style restaurant. Having never visited Alaska, she was serious enough to come north to explore the concept. She came, she saw and she was devastated. She hated Alaska, was depressed by the short, dark, cold days and she was deeply disappointed that what she saw fell short of what she had imagined. There were no log cabins, mountain men, Eskimos or rustic saloons that she hoped to see. With a parting shot at Alaska's shortcomings, she beat a hasty retreat to warm, sunny New Mexico.

Unlike Ernestine, the Flint family enjoyed a thrilling adventure during our four year stay. Almost everyone loves Alaska but sooner or later almost everyone leaves Alaska and hardly anyone stays long enough to die in Alaska. My working life there brought me into close contact with Alaska Native leaders who were aggressively pursuing their land claims against the government. It was interesting to learn of the similarities and differences in the experiences of Native Americans in New Mexico and Alaska. The Alaskans were essentially landless at that time and the New Mexicans had their pueblos and their reservations. Both peoples had suffered at the hands of governments and invaders of their traditional lands, a problem that the Alaskans were to see partly remedied with the passage of the historic Native Claims Settlement Act.

One unforgettable character who was prominent in the long battle for recognition of native claims to Alaska land was Charles Edwardson, Jr., an Eskimo from Barrow. His Eskimo name was Etok. Charlie was Harvard educated but as a young man he was a rowdy, hard drinking guy, usually carelessly dressed and handicapped with a stutter. He was an angry young man on a mission to establish his people's ownership of their ancestral ownership of Alaska's North Slope. I was employed by British

Petroleum, now better known as BP, the company with the largest share of the oil at Prudhoe Bay. As a result, the company and the native people had a coincidental and ironic shared interest. The Alyeska Pipeline from the North Slope to Valdez could not be built until the native claims were settled.

One summer morning two colleagues and I arrived at the garage of BP's Anchorage office building and boarded the basement elevator, headed for the top floor conference room where we were to have a meeting with Charlie and other Eskimo leaders. The elevator stopped at the ground floor where we were warmly greeted by Charlie who joined us with a big smile and said, "Good morning, you fucking corporate pigs!" We knew him well enough to know that this was a friendly greeting and responded with the expected hearty laughs. Later that day after a productive meeting we repeated the story to other members of our team and they too enjoyed a good laugh. As we all retreated to appreciative silence, one of our friends, a usually dour Scottish geologist, commented, "Even if it's true, he shouldn't have said it." None of us will ever forget Charlie Edwardson, either for his brash sense of humor or for his persistence in pursuing the land rights of his people.

After Alaska we moved on to San Francisco for a three year stay. During the seven years of our Alaska and California exile we made frequent visits to New Mexico and sustained our long time New Mexico friendships. By the summer of 1977 my employment had taken us to Cleveland, Ohio. As thoroughly inoculated westerners, we found it hard to move back east. That disappointment was compensated in part by my new job description that gave me responsibility for government relations in the mountain states including New Mexico. That happy turn of events soon made possible a business trip to Santa Fe.

It was during that trip that our friends Booker and Susan Kelly told me of a property they were interested in buying on the Rio de Los Pinos, just below the New Mexico border with Colorado. Booker and I had been classmates in law school. He and another old friend, Forrest Smith, had found the property and wanted to find a way to buy it. Like most young lawyers they were cash poor and looking for a partner to share the cost of this adventure. So it was in the summer of 1977 that we had the chance to join with our old friends in an effort to purchase a special property that Chris and I had never seen. We couldn't immediately find an excuse to rush out to New Mexico and inspect the much touted invest-ment opportunity. Despite that failure of due diligence, but convinced by Booker Kelly's glowing description, we said we would like to be the partners he and Forrest Smith needed. We consulted by long distance tele-phone, Chris and I in Cleveland, and the other partners in Santa Fe. We reached agreement and Booker delivered our offer by telephone to Elizaida Espinosa who lived in Denver. In early September, Mrs. Espinosa and Booker closed the deal in another phone call and a written contract was soon signed. We were ready to celebrate.

Soon after that I managed another business trip to Santa Fe that included a beautiful autumn weekend. My friends Booker and Susan drove me up for an overnight visit to our new place. The last fortyfive minutes of the trip along the Rio de Los Pinos valley were enchanting. We looked out across irrigated fields and watched farmers finishing their hay harvest. We saw numerous pickup trucks over loaded with fire wood making their way down from the Carson National Forest and we admired dozens of the ubiquitous horses that are so beloved by the *Hispano* people. When we reached our property near sundown, I was stunned by the beauty of the canyon, the mountains and the river. The old homestead cabin on the property had no electricity, had not been occupied for many years and was unfit to be used as our bedroom so we rolled out our bed roles on the ground. A camp fire cooked our simple supper and after our meal we wanted to have a further look at the interior of our new second home. We positioned our vehicle so that the headlights shined in through the windows and doors, giving us a shadowed look at the rustic interior.

The traditional homestead cabin had three rooms, each with its own exterior doorway. The decrepit old farm house was a "*jacál*" structure with exterior walls made of vertical, side by side cedar posts set into the ground and rising to ceiling height and originally plastered with adobe mud on the inside and out and it had a pitched tin roof.

The old cabin in 1977.

Our lovely moon lit night was enhanced by a bottle of brandy Booker had brought along to help with our celebration. And celebrate we did, to excess. We could never figure out why he decided on brandy but we surely paid a steep price the next morning. By midmorning Booker and I were well enough to do a walk about, admire the river and soak up the warm fall sun. Susan, on the other hand, was so impaired that she was barely able to raise her head from the blanket she had spread out on the soft meadow grass next to the river. On balance the weekend was a huge success, although I'm pretty sure that all three of us have been sparing in the use of brandy in later years. But it soon turned out that we had another hangover to deal with. This one would require a much longer recovery period. We were going to be obliged to prove in the courts of New Mexico that Elizaida Espinosa was the rightful owner of our new property.

Land titles in northern New Mexico and especially in Rio Arriba County were a mine field. Rural *Hispano* landowners were usually unfamiliar with and didn't use the legal procedures and tools of Anglo American law. They couldn't afford and didn't employ lawyers, seldom made wills and often tried to create their own deeds when passing title. Most of these people traced their title back through ancestors or others who never mastered reading and writing in either Spanish or English. But our vendor was only two generations removed from the original homestead patent holder, her grandfather Juan Bautista Gallegos, so we assumed naively that it would be a simple matter to confirm her title. Booker was so confident that he volunteered to handle the legal matter himself if Forrest Smith and the Flints would agree to pay the modest down payment. We agreed and Booker went to work. And what a piece of work it proved to be. Juan Gallegos had conveyed the property to his daughter Criselda with a deed that seemed solid and uncontestable. Criselda married Francisco Archuleta and by the time of the 1930 census they were living on the property with their eight children. Elizaida, at fourteen, was the oldest. We know that Francisco died the next year at the very young age of thirtysix. His was the only clearly marked grave in the small family *camposanto* just across the river from their house. His simple wooden cross still identified his grave when we came along in 1977. Criselda only survived him until 1938 when she died at the age of forty, survived by nine children. And we should not have been surprised that she died without a will. Sometime after her death, her then adult children made an effort to confirm Elizaida as the owner of the property but their efforts were ambiguous, inconclusive and wouldn't pass legal muster as time would tell. When Booker went to work on the matter in 1977, all but one of Elizaida's siblings, or their heirs, agreed that she was the owner, but the children of one deceased sister contested the matter so Booker was obliged to file a quiet title suit in the District court of Rio Arriba County.

The old cabin in early 1980s.

To his surprise the heirs persisted in their objections and the case went to trial. After a contentious hearing and continuing negotiations, the judge entered a final decree in Mrs. Espinosa's favor in August, 1980, almost three years after our agreement to purchase the property. We thought that would certainly end the matter but on the last possible day, the other parties filled their appeal to the New Mexico Supreme Court. It was mystifying why they would take this step since the value of a complete victory would have probably been less than their attorney fees, but perhaps, as is often the case, it was "a matter of principle." So another year passed as briefs were filed and oral argument to the Court took place. Finally, in July, 1981, the Court confirmed the lower court's decision and we were officially the owners of this cherished but illusive property. Four years after our original agreement, Mrs. Espinosa, by then sixty five years old, began to receive her much delayed mortgage payments. It would be another twelve years before she would be paid in full, but she survived to see that day and to the best of my knowledge, at the time of this writing she is still enjoying life, well into her nineties.

Despite the quiet title suit setback which was especially painful for Mrs. Espinosa, the partners had immediately begun to have the use of the place in 1977. We spent the best part of the next thirteen years preserving and upgrading the old *casita* while some of us occasionally enjoyed its increasing comfort while trying to make a living in far distant places.

We were initially enchanted by the beauty and splendid isolation of the property. And the river. There's something really appealing about a fast moving live stream for New Mexico people. But what made the place special for me were the echoes of the *Hispano* pioneers who settled there in the 1890s and the early 1900s and called their new home Santa Rita. The property is in the upper end of a box canyon through which the Rio de Los Pinos flows. About five miles upstream from our place the canyon narrows and ends in the precipitous Toltec Gorge. The river courses down through the gorge from the high meadows about a thousand feet above. The river's source is a few miles north and west in Colorado's South San Juan Wilderness. After passing through Santa Rita it flows through the tiny New Mexico villages of San Miguel and Los Pinos and the little Colorado village of Ortiz, before joining the Rio San Antonio and meandering into the southern edge of the San Luis Valley. It merges there with the Conejos River that then contributes its waters to the Rio Grande.

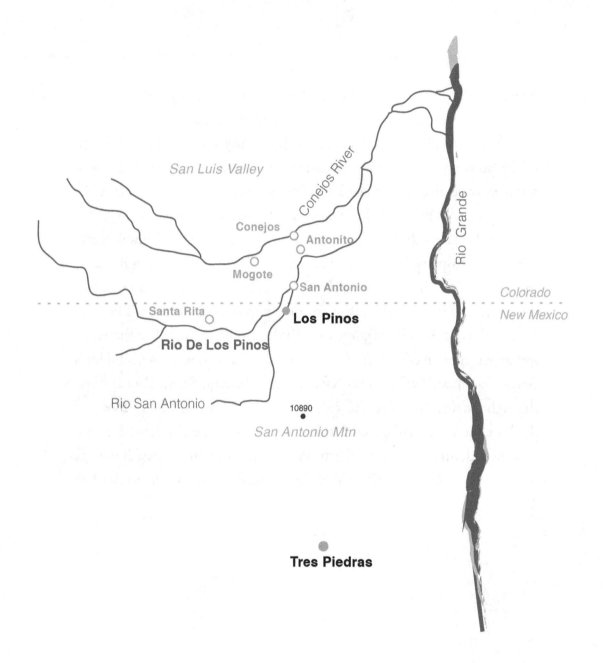

San Luis Valley

Conejos River

Conejos

○ Antonito

○ Mogote

○ San Antonio

Rio Grande

Colorado

New Mexico

Santa Rita ○ ● **Los Pinos**

Rio De Los Pinos

Rio San Antonio

10890
●
San Antonio Mtn

● **Tres Piedras**

Our Santa Rita property is at an elevation of about 8400 feet. To reach it by road from New Mexico it is necessary to drive into Colorado on the highway north from Santa Fe through Ojo Caliente and on up to the neighborhood of Antonito, Colorado. There are two alternate routes to Santa Rita depending on the season, the weather or the whim of the driver. The "high road" is west from Antonito, south at the village of Mogote, over the high ridge between the Conejos River and the Rio de Los Pinos and down a rustic Forest Service road to our place. The "low road" goes west off the highway two miles into Colorado and then up the valley of the Rio de Los Pinos, through two little villages and onto a primitive four mile long Forest Service road that leads to our part of the valley. Both routes required a forty-five minute drive from the main road.

The Santa Rita property straddles the river. On the north side the land rises sharply to cliffs at the skyline and displays scattered junipers and cedars, a few aspens and occasional ponderosas and during the monsoon season, amazing wild flowers. Up on the horizon in the snow free seasons, on the track built by the old Denver and Rio Grande Railroad in 1880, the steam powered Cumbres and Toltec Scenic Railroad train can be seen on its journey from Antonito to Chama and back. On the more protected south side of the river the view is of a similar sharp rise from open meadows to dense stands of aspen, spruce, ponderosas and other conifers. In the center of the valley is the river, bordered by mountain cottonwoods and river willow, surrounded by irrigated meadows. The meadows are watered by *acequias*, hand dug irrigation ditches built by the *Hispano* settlers over a hundred years ago and still maintained by Baudelio Garcia, a grandson of one homesteader and great grandson of another. To the west is the narrowing canyon to the gorge where frequent brilliant sunsets silhouette the massive rock formations upstream from Lobo Creek which drains the eighteen thousand acre Cruces Basin Wilderness. The small inholdings of private land along the river, like ours, are surrounded by the Carson National Forest and the Cruces Basin Wilderness. The property is in Rio Arriba County but only modest services are provided by the folks in the county seat, Tierra Amarilla, which is about one hundred road miles away.

At this location in the upper canyon it was always very quiet. Even the few other private landowners were seldom noticed because of the distance between us and the infrequency of their visits to the valley. Days could go by without seeing other people except the Garcias. Baudelio was almost always in the valley and was a part of our everyday life. By the time we came to the area, there were no longer any full time families living in this part of the valley, although the canyon was still dotted with the old houses and faint traces of the ruins of others that had been the homes of the early *Hispano* settlers.

The only remaining working farmer and rancher in the neighborhood was Baudelio. He and his wife Arlene made their primary home over the north ridge in Mogote, Colorado. Earlier in their lives they had started to raise their two children as full time residents of Santa Rita and as a child, Baudelio lived with his parents and siblings in the old adobe *casita* next door to our old cabin. When we arrived he still grazed his cows in our meadows and in the national forest, irrigated the meadows and harvested the hay from his and our fields. When the snows came in the fall, he opened the field gates and the mother cows trailed their calves up the familiar road over the northern ridge and on to their winter home in Mogote.

When we first met Baudelio in 1978, he was a handsome young man in his middle thirties. He was not a tall man but he always stood tall. Whether he was on a horse, his tractor, in his pickup or on his ATV (all-terrain vehicle) his posture was always erect and his bearing was almost military. He was a man of few words, dignified and reticent, but warm and cordial as he welcomed us as neighbors. Spanish was his first language and he was cautious and sparing in his English conversations with us. He was courteous, generous and discrete, never offering anything but kind words for the newcomers to his valley home. His father preceded him as the *mayordomo* and principal care giver for the many needs of the new people who often faced problems that they couldn't handle on their own. By the time we arrived his father had stepped back from his head man role and Baudelio was taking on his father's responsibilities; providing security, maintaining the five miles of rustic road up the canyon to the last cabin and ready to take on any odd job that the part time residents thought up. As the young guy and his father's son and helper, he was often referred to as "Junior" or "Baldy." When I met him and learned his given name, I thought it was a wonderful name befitting his dignified demeanor and always addressed him as Baudelio.

It would be impossible to overstate the importance of Baudelio's influence on how we viewed our place, its history and our part time life in the valley. He was our bridge to the people and the community that had been there before the rest of us arrived. Without the Garcias we wouldn't have seen the valley as a place where people had once made a living. It would still have been a beautiful and unique get away like many other private refuges of people with the means to carve out a camp or rustic resort, but it would have lacked the real world connections that we enjoyed. The fact that his working farm and ranch surrounded us, his parents' old family home on one side and his own cabin on the other, gave us the gift of proximity. It allowed us to observe and to modestly participate in the way of life that he and Arlene still lived in Santa Rita. That shared space and social connection gave us something different from what was experienced by our mostly Anglo upstream neighbors. And as time passed we were able to be there more often and for longer stays than most of our local friends who had busy lives elsewhere and lived in more distant places like Las Cruces, Denver, Oklahoma and beyond.

Even in the early days of our life there, when we spent most of the year thousands of miles away, when we and our children were back for only a week or ten days each summer, the Garcias were there around us working most of the time but able to socialize with us in the evening or during manufactured spare time. Baudelio introduced our city kids to horses and took our daughter, Tina, on a ride up to the railroad tracks to wave at startled tourists in the observation car of the train on its way to Osier and Chama. He showed our teenage boys how to explore the rugged canyon up to the railroad tunnel cut through the cliffs above the Toltec Gorge, where they had the thrill of running out of the tunnel ahead of the approaching steam engine, its warning whistle echoing in the canyon.

Our children are now adults with children of their own who now see the magical place as a special part of their heritage. And they all have a place in their hearts and their youthful memories for Baudelio, the handsome, soft spoken gentleman cowboy who was a special part of their young lives. He also had the time and inclination to teach Chris and me a rudimentary course in what ranch and farm life was like for Arlene and him. He was used to working alone most of the time and it was amazing what he could do with only his own two hands and his mechanized equipment. But he could occasionally benefit from having the help of even untrained but willing hands; to "Hold that gate steady" or "Hand me that wrench" or "Pull that barbed wire tighter." And those were things I loved to do. They gave me the pleasure of feeling useful. In a way I suppose he was a little like Tom Sawyer "allowing" his young friends to help him whitewash the fence. The difference was that Baudelio genuinely loved his work but was glad to have a little help and a little company. I finally bought my own little four wheeled ATV that allowed me to help herd his cows up and down the canyon. When Baudelio first saw my new transportation, he commented, "Nice horse!"

My description of Baudelio has been uniformly positive although I'm sure he was not an absolute paragon of virtue. No doubt his wife could have given me examples. He had his eccentricities most of which I won't describe here. But one stands out. It was his fascination with fire. He absolutely loved fires. I'm pretty sure it's partly a cultural thing although I haven't researched it. It's certainly a spring thing. That is, when spring comes and the valley is still grey and brown after the long winter, the place is overflowing with old grass, dry bushes and brush that just cry out to be burned. His reaction is partly the rational belief that burning that stuff will be restorative and will provide abundant new growth, fertilized by the ash from the conflagration. So it is a seasonal rite of passage, a celebration of the New Year. But it is more than that. It's exciting, a little dangerous and it is fun, all things that add to its attraction.

So, frequently when we made our first spring trip to the valley, we were met with evidence of arson. Patches of the hills and fields are scorched and scarred and maybe still smoldering. As I have suggested, it wasn't just a Baudelio thing but seemed to be a part of the *Hispano* heritage. If you were to drive up or down Interstate 25 between Albuquerque and Socorro in the spring and look out across the agricultural land by the Rio Grande, you would see evidence of this practice and probably see the smoke from more than one of these pyrotechnic celebrations.

But with Baudelio it was not exclusively a spring time phenomenon. During one August visit to the valley we noticed an accumulation of flammable debris stacked around the trunk of an old cottonwood tree down by the river, right next to the bridge. Just after dark we noticed a bright, shimmering light in that direction. It was a roaring, gigantic fire surrounding the tree with flames leaping about a hundred feet into the dark sky; a show that would put to shame the annual burning of Zozobra at the Santa Fe Fiesta. And the light of that the inferno revealed Baudelio, sitting in his pickup truck in the middle of the bridge, quietly enjoying his work of performance art. The next day he passed it all off as no big deal. "I just wanted to get rid of all that junk."

Baudelio Garcia was the last survivor of what had for a brief time been a lively community of *Hispano* families living in the valley year round, raising a few cattle and sheep, growing a few crops and living a largely subsistence life style. They schooled their children in little one room school houses, two of which still survive. In everything they did they relied very little on cash. The community began to lose population by the 1930s and by midcentury only Baudelio's parents and their children were still there. In the 1970s when we came, many of the old places were owned by Anglo newcomers like us. But the Garcias were an important part of our lives in the canyon. His elderly parents had moved "to town" but continued to enjoy their old *casita* in Santa Rita during the warm days of summer. Baudelio continued to do the things that go with owning cattle. He mended fences, maintained the *acequias* and diversion dams, cut and baled hay, fixed the road, cared for the animals and did the countless other chores that went with the territory.

Getting Started

After a twenty year hiatus, our three children long since out of the nest, Chris and I returned to Santa Fe in 1990 and began to immerse ourselves again in New Mexico life. One of the main joys of having time on our hands was the opportunity it provided to spend more time at our Santa Rita place. At the time of our return the old cabin provided few amenities. We had electricity but no potable water. About two hundred yards up a steep side canyon behind the cabin, hidden in the deep woods, was a good spring that had been used by our *Hispano* neighbors at an earlier time for domestic water. It was rumored that the spring had also been put to use as the location of a moonshine still that contributed to the income and quality of life of the homesteader families. A discarded washing machine tub had been set in the spring to collect water. Plastic tubing was attached to it that extended all the way down the hill to the old neighboring house where it fed into a large plastic garbage can that had been elevated on an outdoor platform connected to the house. Additional hoses from the tank to the kitchen sinks in our two houses provided running water of sorts. The difference in elevation between the water source and the kitchens, plus the elevated tank created enough hydrostatic pressure to give us a modest flow of non-potable water for dish washing and bathing. Our cabin had no inside bathroom but we built a rough outdoor shower stall where we could hang a solar heated water bag under which we and the mosquitos could take a quick chilly shower.

That's probably more than anyone wants to know about our primitive plumbing system but it was very important to us. Over time there were other adjustments to the primitive comforts of our part time residence. For example, we tightened up the interior integrity of the structure in order to keep most of the mice above the ceiling and out of our three rooms. We knew they were still there because we could hear them at night running around over our heads. For a period of time our cat joined us on our visits and after a night-long hunt the poor thing was dusty and exhausted. Our most important improvement was drilling a one hundred eighty feet deep well that provide us with the most delicious water we had ever tasted.

I have mentioned our partners several times but since the three of us and our wives were to enjoy this place together for almost eighteen years before the new cabin enterprise took shape they deserve a better introduction. We were old friends and had enjoyed good times together in the past as we would in the future, but we came from quite different places geographically and in other ways as well. Booker Kelly was the only native New Mexican in the trio. He was born in Santa Fe, the son of Daniel T. and Margaret Gross Kelly. Dan Kelly was a descendant of one of the founders of the widely known and highly successful mercantile enterprise that came to be called Gross, Kelly and Company. His wife Margaret Gross Kelly came from a prominent St. Louis family that provided the first name in the company's title. The Kellys were well connected to the leadership elite of the region, the state and Santa Fe. Booker grew up in Santa Fe and followed in his father's footsteps at Harvard University.

Forrest Smith was born in Nebraska but after his parents divorced when he was quite young, his mother moved back to Topeka, Kansas, where her parents lived. She was a hard working single parent during his childhood years and raised Forrest and his brother in Topeka. Like many others of his generation, Forrest grew up in the shadow of the Great Depression in a family with a tight budget and a lingering awareness of the hard times so recently experienced. When he graduated from high school he heard the siren call "Go west, young man" and came to Albuquerque and the University of New Mexico. He was a keen and successful student, majored in Anthropology and on graduating was awarded a Fulbright Scholarship that provided him with a year at a university in Mexico City. Forrest and I first met and became friends as undergraduates at the University of New Mexico. Booker and I met a few years later as freshmen at the University's Law School. After our graduation, Booker returned to Santa Fe and joined a prestigious law firm that would later bear his name, where he served as a senior partner for the rest of his long legal career.

Forrest, in the meantime, like many anthropology majors, put his good liberal arts degree to work in the business world before he succumbed to the law school itch and returned to New Mexico to earn his law degree. In 1977 when our three paths merged again, he was an associate in Booker's Santa Fe law firm. Because of their modest financial means Chris and I had the opportunity to share in the adventure of making an investment that would yield only psychic income in the years ahead. And what ideal partners the Flints were to invest in recreational property in the wilds of northern New Mexico. We would be able to use the property only about a week each year for the next thirteen years that we spent living primarily in Cleveland, Ohio. It was not until 1990 that we returned to New Mexico and became full time partners for the first time.

In any event, we did share in the use and gradual improvement of the cabin and property over that long period of time, especially after our return to Santa Fe in 1990. Although we were good friends we were seldom at the cabin at the same time. The place was small, had limited amenities and required more intimacy than we found comfortable, so we traded off; your week, their week, our week. We had different styles that had to be blended and we had slightly different visions of what the place should become. Booker tended to resist change, wanted to preserve the rusticity of a fishing camp and, dare I say it, was reticent about spending money on improvements. The rest of us, including his wife Susan, were more open to improvements. We had our separate views on interior design and décor which could occasionally lead to friction. Forrest and his wife Jean, who he married in 1984, wanted to leave their imprint on the place with small items that were special to them but which may not have appealed to the Kellys. Sometimes those special things seemed to disappear, to the displeasure of the Smiths. The Flints, we would like to believe, were more ecumenical and less judgmental, but who knows how the other partners reacted to our eccentricities.

But the real test of our communal enterprise was how to deal with "improvements." Forrest and Jean, Chris and I and even Susan were more ambitious in our suggestions for change. Booker was more deliberate, dragged his heels or advocated delay or further thought. Susan tended to side with the innovators, as we saw it, or the revolutionaries, as Booker perceived it. One rare weekend when the Kellys and the Flints were sharing the cabin, Susan, Chris and I lamented the interior aesthetics of the old place while Booker was out fishing on the stream. The ancient plastered walls were in rough shape with patches of old wall paper here and there and yellowing newspaper pasted to the ceiling boards between the vigas. We knew that Booker would resist the idea of peeling and scrapping the walls and ceiling. Susan thought we should bite the bullet, just do it and let the chips fall where they may.

Then we could ask Baudelio and Arlene to re-plaster the kitchen walls. Susan said "Booker will be really mad but he'll get over it." Who were we to question her assessment of her own husband's reaction to this outrageous decision? With that settled, we immediately set about moving the furniture away from the walls and began to pull down the old wall and ceiling covering while Booker continued to fish, unaware of our treachery.

It was a hell of a mess when he returned and as Susan had predicted he was mad as hell. He ranted and raved and carried on for some time. Susan took the brunt of his attacks but didn't seem too concerned. She gently tried to make Booker see the wisdom of our decision with little effect. Chris and I simply tried to make ourselves as invisible as possible. We were afraid that we had crossed a red line and had permanently damaged our relationship. Booker finished his angry harangue with the words "You have ruined my whole summer" and stormed out of the house. That was the end of our joint weekend in Santa Rita. Chris and I quickly packed up our things and the two families made their way back to Santa Fe. We feared that we had ruptured our friendship. But Susan was right. He got over it. Baudelio and Arlene Garcia made the old house infinitely more beautiful with their wonderful plaster job and we were all happy with the results. The traumatic events of that weekend were never mentioned, except in Booker's absence, and never again did we share a weekend there with the Kellys.

And that brings us back to the place that brought the partners together. It was about fifty acres of land with a half mile of river front. The place impressed itself on all our senses. The visual impact was perhaps most obvious but the sounds, the smells and even the feel of it were also pervasive. The sound of the river was always with us. Other natural sounds included constant bird song except in deep winter, occasional coyote barking and elk bugling and usually the shifting sound of the wind. And then there were the man made sounds of farm equipment, the buzzing of chain saws and of course the sound of voices. And there were the cows.

The rain brought with it the cherished, sweet New Mexico perfume of wet earth. The clean mountain air carried the scent of the pine and spruce forest and, in the fall, the acrid smell of the blooming chamisa. In most seasons we also enjoyed the comforting smell of smoke from our wood burning stoves.

Our still to be described cabin building project focused our senses on the seasonal characteristics of the summer and early fall months. At our latitude and altitude the sky scape was constantly changing. Some days we watched the sun in its course between the eastern and western mountains with not a cloud in the sky. More often there were a few puffy white clouds in the morning, transformed into cumulous giants in midafternoon and then towering black monsters and blinding lightning, crackling thunder and torrential rain that turned our river chocolate brown. More often than not the storms abated abruptly, leaving a brilliant double rainbow in their wake as the sun broke through over the western mountains.

The appearance of the place varied with the seasons. On our first spring visits of a new year, the cottonwoods along the stream were black skeletons against the background of gray meadows. The river was a torrent, building to its peak flow, usually in June, as the deep snow in the San Juan Mountains slowly melted and produced a roaring white water spectacle. We saw evidence of winter visitors to our fenced yard in the form of elk and deer droppings and perhaps a broken fence rail or two. It was not uncommon even in late May to see a soft gray cloud bank drift into the valley from the west and drop six or eight inches of snow that created a shining, white Christmas like scene when the sun returned.

We had a few chances to see the Santa Rita valley in the deep of winter although in most years we part timers were excluded by heavy snow. Our valley neighbor, Baudelio, recalled that when he was a child the snow was often deep enough to cover the fence posts. Our most memorable winter visit was for the millennium New Year's Eve. We arrived with our daughter and her family on a delightful sunny, afternoon, so warm that we could sit comfortably on the porch while our wood stoves warmed the interior of our new cabin. There was almost no snow and the river was a silent, twisting white ribbon of ice meandering through the meadows. We thought that this would be a great place to be if the world was coming to an end as some were predicting. As it turned out, the first day of the new millennium was another perfect day under a cloudless sky after a ten degree night. We walked up the river to the west and found a small pool that remained open because of the fast moving stream. The water looked black against the surrounding ice. To our surprise, the warm sun encouraged a May Fly hatch and we watched in amazement as they emerged from the murky stream and flew off across the meadow to an uncertain fate.

Throughout our years in the valley, whatever the season, what we observed was affected by two disparate influences, one natural and one man made. The natural physical environment was the product of millions of years of geological and climatological modifications. Those forces gave us a lovely narrow valley with a floor, in our neighborhood, of about 8400 feet in elevation, surrounded by a narrow irrigated riparian strip and steep conifer and aspen covered foothills of the San Juan Mountains. In our viewing area the foothills rise to over 9,000 feet. For us the dominant element of the natural environment is the free flowing wild river that courses through the valley making a valiant effort to reach the Rio Grande.

The second aspect of our view is the change to the natural environment accomplished by the people who have come here. Perhaps surprisingly, the first example of man-made change is the track of the narrow gauge railroad built in 1880 by the Denver and Rio Grande Railroad. It still operates as the Cumbres and Toltec Scenic Railroad, co-owned by the states of New Mexico and Colorado. Of course there was human activity here for thousands of years before the railroad became the first human venture to change the face of the valley but the native people who used the place for so long left little physical evidence of their presence.

So the railroad was in the background. In the foreground were the changes produced by the *Hispano* settlers who came to our stretch of the Rio de Los Pinos valley in the late nineteenth and early twentieth centuries. They were among the last representatives of a three hundred year journey, following the little rivers north in a continuing search for a place to make a living. They called this new place Santa Rita and began making the changes that are still evident in the twenty first century. They came as homesteaders, built their rustic houses, several of which survive, usually modified by the late comers like us who might be called life style pioneers. They immediately prepared the arable land for cultivation of the crops that contributed to their subsistence way of life. To irrigate the fields they built eight or ten *acequias*, irrigation ditches that they carved out of the river sides, relying only on man and horse power to get the job done. In our part of the valley two of those *acequias* are still maintained and used by us and Baudelio. He harvests and bales native grass hay from his fields and ours to feed his cattle through the winter. He continually repairs the two diversion dams that keep the water flowing into our fields and during the irrigation season he is busy directing the water to all corners of the meadows. The visual result for those of us who don't rely on the irrigation for a livelihood is a beautiful view sharply divided by the perfectly horizontal line of the *acequias* with everything below it a green velvet carpet and everything above it a typical harsh New Mexico scrub verging up into the tall trees of the Carson National Forest.

The pioneers who came here didn't think of it this way but they were among the last to participate in the centuries long endeavor to extend the boundaries of the *Hispano* homeland which at its peak covered parts of five states. In our little valley, land title records of the Bureau of Land

Management show that twelve homesteaders acquired Homestead Patents on land in the five mile stretch of the valley below Toltec Gorge. The first of them probably set up housekeeping in about 1888 and most of the rest of them had arrived by about 1910.

Despite their small numbers these people had a strong sense of shared identity and they gave their scattered community the name Santa Rita. Their unofficial name for the settlement was even recognized in the 1910 census which grandly described this tiny enclave as "Santa Rita Township." The *Hispano* residents of Santa Rita are long gone except for Baudelio but their heirs in the larger surrounding community still revere Santa Rita as their ancestral home and call it their "*patria chica*." While the people are mostly gone the evidence of their presence is still a vivid part of the scene; *acequias*, diversion dams, irrigated meadows, fallow fields, houses and ruins, *camposanto*s, rusting farm equipment, deteriorating fences, rough roads and trails and old hill side tree stumps.

We were later to learn more of the history of our new property. The fifty acre tract was originally acquired under the terms of the Homestead Act by one of the early *Hispano* settlers in the valley. He was Juan Bautista Gallegos and early census records informed us that he was born in about 1855, just seven years after American sovereignty was established. We don't know where he was born but we do know that in 1875 he married

Abelina Ruybalid who was born in Ojo Caliente, New Mexico in 1857. We don't know how and when they found their way to our valley but the Gallegos Homestead patent on the land was issued in 1912. We do know that, as was the case with many of the early settlers in the valley, they had established their residency on the property at a much earlier date. The old house on the property was almost certainly the original homestead residence of the Gallegos family and was later owned by Elizaida Espinosa, a granddaughter of Juan Gallegos. My book, *Hispano Homesteaders; The Last New Mexico Pioneers, 1850–1910* recounts the history of the settlement in our valley that became known as the community of Santa Rita.

Elizaida had "inherited" the place from her mother, Criselda Archuleta, a daughter of the original homesteader, Juan Gallegos. The land we had acquired and the vast stretch of territory that encompassed all the little villages and open space in this part of northern New Mexico and all the land and settled places in the southern San Luis Valley of Colorado were within the boundaries of what ultimately proved to be a failed Mexican land grant. The Conejos Grant was made by Mexican Governor Francisco Serracino in 1833, to about forty families and later revalidated to include over eighty families. Each family was granted land for their individual use (called *suertes*) and the vast remainder of the grant, surely including Santa Rita Canyon, was to be the Spanish equivalent of the commons, (called the *ejido*), to be used by the community in perpetuity for grazing, hunting and fishing and for timber and fire wood harvesting. The grantees and their heirs pursued their rights to the grant property for almost a hundred years, but the American legal system defeated their efforts and the grant was ultimately rejected in full by the American courts. One ironic result of this outcome was that the *Hispano* settlers in Santa Rita, like thousands of others throughout the territory, came to rely on the Homestead Act to acquire lands that their ancestors may well have had a claim to under Mexican law, property rights that the United States was obliged to honor under the terms of the Treaty of Guadalupe Hidalgo that ended the American war with Mexico.

During the first four years after our return to full time residence in New Mexico, we shared the cabin with our friends and partners, trading visits and working to make the old place more comfortable, efficient and homey. But with the passage of time and the inconvenience of moving in and out in turn, we came to realize that we would enjoy having our own place. We all loved the old cabin but something had to give.

Since the Harlan Flints were officially "retired" and Booker Kelly and Forrest Smith were still gainfully employed, it was decided that the Flints would consider creating a second cabin. During the winter of

1994–1995 we agonized over the decision and brainstormed the question of how to make it happen. To say that my construction experience was limited would be a gross exaggeration. I had never built anything more complicated than a small book case in a seventh grade shop class. Does anyone remember what a shop class was? So the challenge was daunting. What kind of house could we realistically expect to build, considering our uninspiring credentials?

Adobe was of course an appealing option but the basic ingredients would be difficult and time consuming to make or very expensive to buy. We were inspired by reading many books about adobe architecture, including *La Casa Adobe* by the distinguished Santa Fe architect and artist William Lumpkins, who coincidentally had designed the house we had recently bought in Santa Fe. But we were intimidated by the skills and artistry of the old masters. Besides it would take forever, be expensive and not very energy efficient.

The original *Hispano* settlers in the area had usually bypassed adobe bricks, instead using the abundant, locally available timber to build notched log houses when they homesteaded here. We considered that possibility but we didn't have access to local logs and the idea of building a kit log house was unappealing, very expensive and, again, not very energy efficient. I suppose we could have built a conventional frame stucco house but that implied carpentry skills we couldn't aspire to and the idea was offensive from an aesthetic standpoint considering the cultural and physical environment of our building site.

Then, almost miraculously, along came a book in 1984 that settled the issue for us. That inspiring book was *The Straw Bale House* by Athena Swentzell Steen, Bill Steen, David Bainbridge, with David Eisenberg. Athena Swentzell Steen told of dealing with the same challenge we faced when she and her husband were preparing to build a house on Glorieta Mesa, near Santa Fe. She said they were looking for something fast, easy, warm and inexpensive. The introduction to their book really made the case for straw bales. "They are super energy efficient, simple to work with and can be used both inexpensively and aesthetically." What more could you ask for? And the authors convinced us that we were smart enough to build a straw bale house with only limited assistance. We were sold.

During that winter after we had committed to straw bales, we began to design the house in our imagination and on paper. It was clear that we needed professional help and we turned to Tony Perry, a Santa Fe enthusiast and straw bale expert to take our rough ideas and turn them into working drawings. By spring we were ready to go. But we needed helping hands with a project of this size and turned to our Santa Rita neighbor and friend, Baudelio Garcia. He had great common sense, a wealth of problem solving experience and a tractor, a front end loader and back hoe and a road grader. These were all things that would come in handy for amateur builders. We met with him and his wife, Arlene, and sorted out the details of our working relationship. It was agreed that he and I would undertake the challenge of getting our house under roof by the fall of 1995.

In the early spring while the snow was still on the ground we paced the ground to the east of the old cabin and roughly settled on the footprint of the new cabin. It was on high ground between two small arroyos.

Up canyon view from new cabin site. March, 1995.

It had a splendid view up the canyon and had good access to electric power to be provided by the Kit Carson Rural Electric Co-op and water to be provided by the well we and our partners had drilled at the old cabin.

Other commitments and a long slow spring delayed our official construction kick off until early June. We had studied the plans and could imagine the possibility of executing them but we faced the prospect with some trepidation and uncertainty. The long months ahead would bring us all the magic, hope, fear, frustration, triumph, personal growth, friendship, pride and satisfaction that can be experience by people engaged in that most human of all work, building our own house. And we were building it in a place surrounded by reminders of the even more intense experience of the *Hispano* homesteaders who began their settlement in this valley about a hundred years earlier.

From the Ground Up

By early June, we had done all we could to prepare ourselves for the work ahead. On June 4 the ceremonial "first shovel" was dug with Baudelio Garcia's road grader. How many people have a friend who has a road grader? This ancient machine was long retired from the Conejos County Road Department and it was used to begin leveling the hillside and create a flat place to build our house. I had decided to keep a journal to record our progress. On that important first day of work my journal reported that, "It was a cool, early spring day, cold enough for a down vest and jacket during the afternoon rain storm. Pretty sunset. High river. Lots of snow up above. We saw a couple of big fat deer and a few elk this evening."

It was a long way from this beginning to a completed straw bale house, but we were started. Since this story is to be about a straw bale house, perhaps a brief discussion of straw bales and straw bale construction would be helpful. Straw is the byproduct or waste product from harvesting grains such as wheat, barley or oats. The grains are cut in the field and processed by a threshing machine, sometimes called a combine, which separates the seed or grain from the stems of the plant. The remnant straw was traditionally treated as waste and was often burned in the field or plowed back into the soil. In recent times it is usually baled and usefully put to work by highway departments and others to control soil erosion or used as bedding for animals. Hay, on the other hand is cut and dried alfalfa or other grasses, baled with the seeds and used as animal feed.

Straw bales have been used as construction materials for ages, particularly in the late nineteenth century in farm communities in the upper states of the American Midwest and before that in Europe. Straw bale construction enjoyed a renewal in the late twentieth century and has been enthusiastically adopted in New Mexico as an easy, efficient and environmental friendly alternative to conventional building methods. In the design plans for our cabin the bales were not to be weight bearing. The structure would be supported by posts and beams and the bales would be stacked in the spaces between the posts to create the exterior walls of the house. This story is devoted mostly to the experience of building the house and not to the technical challenges of construction but as we move along we will occasionally get into the nitty gritty details. At this stage it is sufficient to say that building with straw bales is easier and cheaper than working with other materials such as brick, adobe, logs, concrete blocks and standard frame construction. And, based on our experience, it's more satisfying and more fun.

One key advantage of straw bales, especially in a high, cool mountain area subject to extreme weather, is their remarkable insulation quality. Energy efficiency of walls is measured by something called the R-value. Studies show that walls made with bales such as we used have an R-value of about 45, which is perhaps three times greater than wall systems in a conventional home. But, that's enough science for now. Let's move on to the human experience of building our house in the wilderness of New Mexico's northern mountains.

The jointly owned old cabin was our base of for operations during the construction year. The first photo shows an early spring view of the old cabin taken from a position close to where the new house was to be built.

View of old cabin from new building site.

The next picture was taken on the first day of actual work and shows preliminary site preparation using the road grader and front end loader. It was to be a long, slow job and much of it needed to be done with hand tools. While that work continued sporadically, the two big items on our priority list were straw bales and a concrete contractor. The house was to be built on a concrete slab and a contract for that work would be the biggest item in our budget. The straw bales would not be needed for some time but it was not too early to worry about where we would find them. All of our shopping was a challenge. Our permanent residence was in Santa Fe, about one hundred and thirty five miles and two hours and forty-five minutes away. More locally, our building site was over an hour's drive to the nearest hardware and building supply store in La Jara, Colorado. For other supplies we had to drive another fifteen miles north to Alamosa, Colorado. These circumstances indicate how important it was for us to plan ahead.

Early June site preparation.

We started right away. Baudelio was our guide and advisor as we navigated the new, unfamiliar territory. One early morning we picked him up at his Mogote home and headed for La Jara and Alamosa. We had little idea of where to shop for bales so we asked questions. Several leads proved to be dead ends. One straw bale impresario said that all the bales he could find from the 1994 crop were committed to the Colorado Highway Department. Another possibility, a farmer friend of Baudelio's, wasn't home in the village of Capulín when we dropped by. So we moved on to our other priority, finding a concrete contractor who could install our foundation and slab, something we would need quite soon. To make a short story shorter, we wandered around Alamosa, made a couple of phone calls and found a contractor, Bob McGuire, who seemed highly qualified, nice, interested and available, "probably in a few weeks." He was challenged by the journey to our place but seemed willing to chance it. Until we found Bob, we were beginning to feel a bit discouraged. Finding him was one of the many small miracles that would be necessary to make this project go.

There was still much to be worked out, including price and how to get huge concrete mixer trucks up into the mountains on rustic roads and down a very rough, narrow, steep Forest Service road to our place, almost forty miles away. But we worked it out and we had a deal. The straw bale issue was also quickly resolved. Baudelio's friend, Lionel Valdez, was prepared to sell and deliver three hundred bales for $1.50 per bale, a very good price.

While the new house was our top priority, the needs of the valley could not be ignored. Baudelio was a farmer and rancher and our combined irrigated meadows supplied the hay required to carry his cows and calves through the long winter. The river had just reached its peak run off from the heavy winter snows and the *acequia* on the other side of the river was in desperate need of repair, so we interrupted our project to deal with that problem. There were a couple of huge breaks in the *acequia* walls, one caused by elk coming down from the mountains, trampling and breaking the ditch bank, the other caused by a beaver dam and the resulting accumulation of water that washed out the *acequia* wall. We shoveled, tossed rocks and dirt, cleaned out willow bushes, covered the major break with fallen logs and old roofing tin and got the ditch running.

There were always competing demands on our time. It was important that we bring electricity to the building site as soon as possible. We had found a wonderful combination plumber and electrician in Poquaque who would work weekends to meet our needs. He pre-rigged a twenty foot power pole that would allow us to connect to the electrical service provided to our remote valley by The Kit Carson Electrical Coop, out of

Taos. Chris and I borrowed Baudelio's truck and horse trailer to collect the pole on a quick trip to Santa Fe. On the return trip we came in on the high road that took us down over the 9,000 foot high ridge to the north of our cabin and into our valley below. It was a slow drive down the rough road, pulling the big horse trailer. About half way down the hill towards the river we caught up with an old pickup truck with a trailer, both heavily loaded with some of our straw bales. They were parked, blocking the road, and no one was in sight. There was no sign of trouble except that the pickup looked totally over loaded and was way down on its springs. Chris used the delay as an excuse to walk the rest of the way down the hill, which she preferred to riding down with me. I took a short rest in the truck. After a few minutes I heard Baudelio's John Deere tractor chugging up the hill. He arrived with his friend and our bale provider, Lionel Valdez, a young farmer and part time snow plow driver for the Colorado Highway Department. Lionel had felt insecure about his brakes on that last steep pitch and had unloaded his wife and three children to walk to the bottom. He and Baudelio went for the tractor to belay the truck and trailer down the most treacherous part of the mountain road. A chain was connected between the tractor and the back end of Lionel's trailer and we all headed off down the mountain at a stately pace, an imposing caravan to be sure. At the bottom, out in Baudelio's meadow were Lionel's wife, Michelle, and their three small children, waving us in as if we were an arriving cruise ship. We came to a stop and Baudelio unhooked the chain. It was a pretty wimpy chain. Lionel looked at it for the first time and said, "I have a dog that could break that chain." But it had served the purpose of providing psychological reinforcement as the overloaded rig moved safely down the mountain, and that was what Baudelio had in mind. We three men then unloaded the 150 bales while Chris served a light lunch for the women and children. We also unloaded the power pole and had a cold beer after which Lionel and family and Baudelio headed back to Colorado to load the other 150 bales. Chris and I drove back to Santa Fe for the weekend, proud owners of 300 stout straw bales.

MONDAY, JUNE 12

Tonight is one of those special nights that tempt an observer to describe their beauty. An unanticipated full moon that seems to leap into the brightened eastern sky at 8:30 looks twice as big as the next biggest moon I've ever seen. The twin lights of the huge moon and the setting sun reveal the dim outline of six elk grazing on the other side of the river, a river still swollen and noisy from the late snow melt.

Earlier, when the sun was high, Baudelio used his backhoe to dig a 100 yard trench from the well and power pole, close to the old cabin, up to the new cabin. I was following him with a five foot measure to insure that the trench was deep enough to protect the water line from the winter cold. Just as in the city, it is mesmerizing to watch men working with heavy equipment, in this case a backhoe, cutting through surprisingly soft, black dirt that has washed down over thousands of years from those old cliffs to the north. Across the river is a feature not often seen in nature; what seems to be an absolutely perfect horizontal line. It is the soft but distinct path of the *acequia*, almost exactly parallel with the circumference of the earth, a line dictated by laws unfamiliar to the people who created it with sweat and shovels 90 or 100 years ago. That line is not out of place in the natural scene. Rather, it enhances and balances a picture that hasn't been spoiled by the presence of man. It's kind of like the green, wild but softly domesticated beauty of the English Lake District where the mark of man's presence is more accurately attributable to sheep. On a more prosaic note, we also installed our power pole today, perfectly perpendicular, as attested by the bubble in our carpenter's level.

The rest of June was a busy time with little obvious tangible evidence of progress. We continued to struggle with defining and leveling the building site, a process that required much hand and machine work. Another project was the construction of a combined storage shed and outhouse, a vital component of our long endeavor.

The outline of the foundation was marked with a chalk line and we excavated a trench along the edges to prepare for pouring the footers and installing the concrete forms for the stem walls.

We had borrowed a surveyor's transit from our contractor and taught ourselves how to use it to fix good levels for the foundation. The weather stayed very spring-like with night time temperatures in the thirties, cool days, occasional thunderstorms and lots of mosquitos. By June 30, our contractor, Bob McGuire, had put in the foundation footers and his workers had built the forms for the concrete stem walls. In the meantime we had taken our working drawings to the La Jara Trading Post, our closest hardware store and lumber yard and asked them to do a "take off" estimate of the cost for all the building materials required to complete our project. By this time we were ready for our first big concrete pour.

July 6. First pour.

July 6 was a red letter day. At 9:00 a.m. the men from McGuire and Sons arrived and at 10:00 the big cement mixer came cautiously down the high road with a six yard load of concrete for the stem walls. By noon their work was done and they were gone. Baudelio came by to report on the Fourth of July activity in the valley. The big news for our neighbors was that there had been a huge "Rainbow Family" gathering a few miles away in the Carson National Forest, just west of Tres Piedras, New Mexico. There had been some concern that this giant festival of ex-hippies might spill over into our valley. But none of the Rainbow people breached our security lines. There were reported to be over 15,000 people camped out in the Forest. A centerpiece of their celebration was an hour long noon time period of silence, an extended prayer for world peace. It worked, at least in our neck of the woods. A few days after the stem wall pour the McGuire crew were back to remove the wood forms and reveal the completed stem walls.

Stem walls with exposed rebars.

A close look at the photo shows lengths of rebar that had been inserted into the wet concrete and that extended vertically above the foundation walls. When the time came to start building the straw walls, the first two courses of bales would be pressed down over the rebars to stabilize the straw walls.

By this time, in the middle of July, many things were happening at once. After the under the slab work was done, we had to import clean fill dirt to bring the level up to four inches below the top of the stem walls to accommodate the four inch thick slab. We were also shopping for lumber, windows, doors and other supplies to be delivered by our friends at La Jara Trading Post. And we met with our building design contractor to agree on interpretation of ambiguous elements of the working drawings and to have him answer our questions on how to proceed with the next steps.

THURSDAY, JULY 13

With the plumbing and electrical stuff underground inside the foundation perimeter, we can now bring back McGuire and his troops to pour the slab next week. Then we'll be ready to get above ground. I spent an hour with Tony Perry, our design advisor, going over the plans and improving my understanding of how to do things and how to sequence the work. It's a very complicated business but the next thing to be done, looked at in isolation and considered in collaboration with other fallible human beings, is less daunting. In fact it may be a lot less challenging than the hard physical labor of following Baudelio in his front end loader, distributing by shovel the dirt he is producing with his machines. With the help of his machinery we have a new appreciation for how hard it must have been to get things done up here in the wilderness when Baudelio's grandparents and the other pioneers were here, surviving and prospering, in a way, with little cash and no mechanical help.

Despite the progress made by the middle of July, we were still working in the dirt. We had decided to use a composting toilet which eliminated the need for a septic tank but we still needed a French drain to receive the gray water from the kitchen and bathroom. One dark and cloudy Monday we went to La Jara to shop for PVC pipe and connectors to complete the sewer line to the deep hole filled with large rocks that we called the French drain. The Trading Post was a minimalist supplier of plumbing supplies and sure enough, back at the building site, the parts we had purchased wouldn't turn the corners we needed to turn. Besides, it had started to rain and everything was turning to glue in the trench. It was impossible to finish the job without additional fittings and that would mean a trip to Alamosa, about a three hour round trip.

As we faced that dilemma, along came Baudelio with a young man who was the brother of one of our valley neighbors. It appeared that he was to be in the valley for the summer, caring for his brother's place and anxious to find gainful employment. The two of them volunteered to go on a search for the needed supplies. Late that afternoon, our new friend, Brian, drove up to our old cabin in a very muddy utility vehicle and reported that after many stops in Alamosa and places in between they had found the necessary pieces. He accepted our invitation for dinner, in the course of which we talked about our project and negotiated an off-the-books contract for his services at $8.00 an hour with no benefits except free beer and an occasional meal. Our work crew was now complete.

TUESDAY, JULY 18

A very good day. Chris and I laid the sewer line this morning before our new helper showed up for work. It was by far the best sewer line we've ever installed! Baudelio and Brian appeared at about 11:00, ready to back fill some of our many ditches. Brian excused his late arrival, claiming that it was my fault because I had loaned him our straw bale book and he had stayed up reading until 2:30 in the morning. He's now a convert to this new technology. The rest of our day was consumed by the trench filling work, both inside and outside of the foundation. We also touched up the surface level where the slab was soon to be poured. The building site is now a thing of beauty, at least in the eyes of those who did the work. It's hard to remember what it looked like when Baudelio first tore into it with the road grader and front end loader. The McGuire crew will certainly be impressed and will probably want us to join their team. But, NO WAY! This is definitely our last foundation prep job. We finished right at 4:30, when if he had been here, Winnie the Pooh would have exclaimed "It's time for a little something!" So we all returned to the old cabin and had a couple of beers that tasted fantastic. We also discussed cook stoves, composting toilets, elk hunting and snow machining but not a word about Bosnia, Newt Gingrich or Bill Clinton.

WEDNESDAY, JULY 19

This place is rich with life this summer. The river is down now but the meadows are wet and exploding with growth. If you walk down to Baudelio's cabin in the evening as Chris and I did last night, the full length of the power line is packed with swallows, most of them just watching the sunset and not eating enough mosquitos. During our work day the mosquitos are in thick swarms, especially during the frequent rain showers. Sometimes it's even difficult to avoid inhaling them. I try to breathe through my teeth! But they are fairly heavy footed dudes. You feel them land and can usually kill or disperse them before they bite. There are wild flowers everywhere, from big patches of Indian paintbrush up on the high road to all manner of wild roses, lilies and other wild flowers. The dry looking hillsides to the north are covered with extravagant, bright spears of yucca blossoms. And that's just the species we can put a name to. It's a good thing the concrete guys didn't come in today. I had forgotten that I need to place rigid foam insulation under the slab, next to the foundation, about three hours of work.

The next day the concrete crew came in to make final preparations. They moved in a little more dirt to raise the grade. They also installed steel wire mesh to reinforce the concrete and said they would be back to pour the next day.

Final preparation for pouring slab.

Early the next morning the advance crew arrived early. Then a little while later the big event started. It took three cement trucks carrying a combined seventeen yards of concrete to do the job and the three trucks arrived in sequence, like clockwork, to keep the finishers busy. It was a beautiful day and a grand sight for the spectators who stood and watched the whole operation.

After they finished and the trucks were on their way back to Alamosa, I made one of my frequent journeys to La Jara for a few items we would need the following week. On my way back in, near Atencio Springs on the high road, I came across the two men who had been doing cement finishing. Their truck was parked and they were out in the field beside the road, each carefully examining the ground at their feet. It turned out that they were arrow head collectors and were taking the chance to search in new territory. It would not be surprising to find arrow heads or other Native American artifacts here. For thousands of years this area and the entire San Luis Valley to the north had been the home of many native peoples. The Indians were long gone, having been forced out of their homeland and onto reservations in the late nineteenth century and there was little evidence, beyond the occasional arrow head, of their ancient presence.

The big milestone for us on Friday, July 21, was that after almost two months, the foundation was finished. We were out of the dirt and ready to use the platform we had created to start the real work of building our handmade house in the wilderness.

A beautiful day to pour the slab.

Raise High the Roof Beams

Now that we are about to describe the beginning of the actual above ground construction process, it may be a good time provide a little more detail about the building design and the management of the project, if it can be dignified with that term. We had been provided with working drawings by Tony Perry of Straw Bale Construction Management, Inc., in Santa Fe. The plan described a building with outside dimensions of 45 feet by 27 feet. The total design package was contained in three pages; the Main Floor Plan, the Foundation Plan and the Roof Framing Plan, plus a few written specifications. The perimeter posts and beams would to be the only weight bearing feature and would support the roof comprised of pre-fabricated roof trusses, plywood panels and sheathed with a metal pro panel covering. The forty five by twenty seven foot shape of the house was influenced by the three foot long dimension of the bales. The bales were to be in-filled between the posts and were to be laid flat, with the vertical joints staggered at each course. Each course of bales was to be reinforced with two vertical rebar pins inserted through each bale and into the underlying bale. A continuous flexible horizontal truss-like frame, called Dura Wall was to be placed between each course of bales and tied to the bale twine for additional stability. We will talk about the challenge of doors and windows when their time comes.

In terms of project management, I would probably have to be described as the foreman, since I knew more about the design details than my co-workers. In reality however our working relationship could better be described as collaborative. It was my job to look at the plans and the job each evening and plan for the next day and the next week. The simple plans contained some ambiguity but the solutions were usually within our combined capabilities. My main partner, Baudelio, was already a creative and trusted old friend and our new worker, Brian Ackelson, was capable and skilled and had a good work ethic. We were also fortunate to have superb contractors with whom Baudelio, Brian and I merged seamlessly. The same could be said for our principal supplier, La Jara Trading Post, where we were always warmly greeted and competently advised whenever we dropped in for supplies and advice.

During our time together on and off the job, we three collaborators, with Chris's support, worked hard when we worked but we were not driven by artificial deadlines. We accepted the inevitable interruptions and detours. The experience was enjoyable and our relationship was cordial and congenial. We respected one another and each partner contributed invaluable insights and suggestions. It was a happy time for all of us. And, what a place it was to be and to work. Soon after the slab pour, we went to work fabricating and installing the site built columns or posts that would support the house. Lag bolts had been inserted into the wet foundation cement to be used to connect the columns to the foundation.

Site built columns being installed.

Baudelio, Brian and I installed most of the support columns in one day. One evening about that time, after one of our many jaunts to La Jara, we were on our way back into the valley on the high road when the muffler on our old Jeep fell off. The resulting unmuffled engine gave me a real sense of power as the four cylinder engine sounded like a Boeing 747 jet. So, a little after noon the next day, Chris and I drove to La Jara in two separate vehicles, the outspoken Jeep and Baudelio's more discreet pickup. We went to the non-franchise muffler shop and described our problem. Without even glancing at our Jeep, the shop owner took our keys (no paper work) and said, "Come back anytime you want to tomorrow." That done, we went over to do our shopping with Dan Bond, the harried manager of the Trading Post, who would rather build things with his own hands than deal with the paper work of running a late twentieth century business in a small Colorado town. He concluded his session with us saying," I have a nervous stomach and it's getting more nervous all the time."

I previously mentioned the rebar pins used to stabilize the bale walls. We needed about 225 of them, each 30 inches long, to be driven through the top course of bales and into the course below. Dan Bond thought he knew of a man who had a rebar cutter and lived in Mannassa, home town of Jack Dempsey, the Mannassa Mauler. After a couple of trips and phone calls we found Juan Cisneros in Antonito. He loaned us his device which allowed us to buy long rebars and cut them into the desired lengths.

The next day we reached another milestone. We had constructed the four perimeter beams, two of them 45 feet long and two that were 27 feet long. The question was how to raise high the roof beams and place them on top of the support columns. Baudelio studied the problem after he went back to his cabin for the night and came up with an imaginative solution. When we arrived in the morning, he had arranged three oil drums at the edge one of the long walls.

We placed the beam along that wall and we three positioned ourselves next to the barrels, lifted the beam and placed it on top of the barrels. Then each of us stood on our barrel and, on command, hoisted the beam and settled it on top of the support columns. Having met that challenge, it was a relatively simple matter to complete the post and beam structure that would support the whole house.

"Garcia solution." Raising perimeter beams.

Over the following weekend we spent some time getting excited about future contents for the house, such as the Stanley wood cook stove from Waterford, Ireland, plus a smaller wood stove for one of the bedrooms, and the planned composting toilet. All of these items and a few others had been ordered from the wonderful Lehman's Non-Electric Hardware Store in Kidron, Ohio (Amish country), largest supplier of such traditional products in the United States. When I called the Lehman people to place the order, they were awestruck to hear that the shipping destination would be La Jara Trading Post in small town Colorado, probably one of the most remote sales in their history.

The beginning of August brought us not only a new month but also the new adventure of actually building with straw bales. We had begun to store the bales inside the structure in anticipation of this new stage. We discussed how to spread black plastic roofing cement on the edge of the slab and how to cut and position visqueen which would be placed under and around the outside of the first course of bales to protect them from moisture.

Bringing in the bales.

Black plastic and Visqueen Moisture Protection.

WEDNESDAY, AUGUST 2

Brian, being young and strong, believed intuitively in brute force. Even though the bales are compacted by a powerful machine, he is convinced that if you try hard enough you can squeeze 16 inches of bale into 14 inches of space. Most of our walls are looking good but one is bowed out because we packed the bales in too tight, causing the wall to be distorted. Brian just stopped by on his way to town and agrees that he's worried about the wall and knows it has to be fixed. I think we should take it down partially and rebuild it right. He thinks that if we attach a "come along" to a board behind the wall we can pull it into shape. I'm no physicist but I don't think that will work.

We fixed the wall the right way and Brian was gracious in endorsing that solution. Part of the problem with the wall was where we had placed the rough frame for a window in the north wall of the living room. We changed the location when we rebuilt the wall. One of the benefits of this kind of construction is that changes of that sort can be made easily without complications.

We had been blessed by having no rain since we started bringing in the bales that had been stored at Baudelio's cabin. We had hoisted some seventy five bales off Baudelio's truck and trailer and stacking them inside the house. One of the few downsides of straw bale construction is having loose straw inside your shirt, underwear, socks, mouth and nose, especially on a hot, dry day. The end of the day shower was positively mind altering.

One of the recurring themes of this narrative is the need for frequent, often unscheduled shopping trips, most of them shared with our working partner, Baudelio. It was a treat and a lesson to go to Antonito, La Jara and Alamosa with him. It was one of the many experiences that added to our appreciation of his wisdom and savvy. He was well known and respected in town, especially by the many other *Hispano* people we dealt with. He was quiet and unassuming but definitely not a push over. He knew our agenda and knew how to get things done. That often meant that he got us to do and say the things we were supposed to do and say without actually telling us what they were. It kept us on our toes to be constantly inferring his intentions based on subtle hints and cryptic verbal signals. It was always comforting to be with someone who was "someone" in these less familiar places. We had the feeling that sometimes the other folks were wondering what the hell he was doing with us and he didn't answer their unasked questions, leaving them to worry and speculate about it with their families at the end of the day.

This phenomenon was just a part of our fundamental compatibility as a working group. Our friendship was not threatened by the necessity to work together in a business like way. It helped bridge any occasional disagreements that are inevitable when friends feel free to differ on the best way to get from here to there. This is not always true when people of different skills, life experiences and cultures engage in the emotionally charged activity of building a house and home for one of the participants in the process. Two recent books brought that home to me. One was *House born of Mud, A Builder's Story* by William N. Gates. The other was *Bird Cloud* by Annie Proulx. Both authors are profoundly accomplished writers whose genius for language and storytelling I admire and envy. But their experiences building their own homes are not ones I would want to emulate. They both set their sights very high, perhaps unrealistically. In Gates' case, he may have come amazingly close to what he had hoped for but only after a tortuously long and difficult path. Annie Proulx described an equally difficult journey that still fell short of what she hoped to achieve. Perhaps just as important, in both stories, their relationships with architects, designers, builders, contractors, craftsmen, suppliers and other employees were often sour and disappointing. Getting there was definitely not half the fun. In both stories there were occasional transcendental achievements, but there was also a persistent legacy of disappointment, disillusion and even sadness. In both books, the long sought after goal of a house and home that would satisfy and nurture the owner, perhaps forever, fell short of expectations and both authors soon gave up the houses they had labored and dreamed over for so long. One cannot regret that the true stories fell short of what had been hoped for. Life is not always perfect. We were perhaps more fortunate in our smaller, less ambitious project. In our case, the place, the process and the end result were deeply satisfying. We and our still expanding family continue to enjoy the cabin and its beautiful and historic environment and we are still close to many of the people who helped make it happen.

FRIDAY, AUGUST 4

Baudelio is away for a few days and Brian and I are settling into a good routine. He does what he does and I do what I do. He does the more physical stuff like shaping bales for the top row and lifting them up there. I do some of the more patient, detail work like putting in the Dura-Wall, stacking bales and inserting the rebar pins. Brian now takes pride in creating the perfect bale, and they are great, shaved down to the exact thickness with a big chain saw and tied in both directions to give them maximum stability and firmness. We don't talk a lot but our silence is cordial. He's had to make every top bale shorter, top to bottom, and that's hard work. No more trying to put a 16 inch bale into a 14 inch space. We both feel better about it. A big challenge in straw bale construction is taking the time to get it right. Another is being prepared to keep the bales dry when it rains.

It hasn't, but it could. I think I'll buy more tarps. We'll probably spend more on tarps than we did on bales but they're adding value to the bales. The worst thing would be to be careless about the bales after we've gone to all the trouble of putting them into the house. I spent an extra hour and a half fine tuning the tarps in case of rain. We're about half done with the walls and rough door and window openings.

Tarps and the threat of rain.

Bale walls half done. Note Visqueen over first course of bales.

In the new week the three of us continued with the walls. I called La Jara Trading Post to let them know we would need the roof trusses soon. One evening the Garcias invited us all to dinner at their cabin down the road. The mosquitoes weren't bad while the sun was still up but when it started to go down they were voracious.

Brian had gone down to Antonito after work but returned in time for the feast. When I saw his costume for the evening I couldn't help thinking he was almost a parody of how he sees himself: levis, running shoes, tank top that shows off his bronzed shoulders, seven beaver Stetson, camouflage jacket and a clip of 30 caliber cartridges in his belt. He was a hell of a hale fellow well met type and despite his approach to charisma, a pretty okay guy. But the brash, exaggerated machismo said everything about his sense of self.

Shortening a bale using bale needle.

We have made frequent mention of the adaptability of straw bales to the differing dimensions required by the plans. That is, the size and shape can be modified to fit the space they would occupy. The most common alteration on our project was to reduce the horizontal width of the bales.

Because the bales would fall apart if the twine ties were cut, it was necessary to resize and retie the new shape before the original ties were cut. In effect we made a new, smaller bale out of the full sized bale. To do this we fashioned what is called a bale needle from a quarter inch steel rod about thirty inches long. One end of the rod was hammered flat and filed down to a point. A small diameter hole was then drilled in the flat point, just large enough to insert the end of piece of polypropylene twine, similar to that originally used to tie the bale. The other end of the rod was bent at a 90 degree angle to form a 6 inch handle. We then marked the two original twine ties at the points where the bale was to be divided. The bale needle with the twine attached was then thrust through the bale at the marked place and the twine was pulled through from the other side, wrapped around the "new" bale and retied at the point where the needle was inserted.

After repeating the process with a second piece of twine, the original two twines could be cut and the excess bale end was easily separated from the new, narrower bale. I promised that I wouldn't get into the technical niceties of our work and this will be a rare exception to that rule, but it was such a satisfying process that I couldn't resist.

On another day shortly before the bale walls were finished, we ran out of rebars so we were off to La Jara again. This time we bought long rebars and cut them to size with a hack saw. Before making the trip, our work was interrupted by rain for the first time. It was a good hard rain and put lots of water inside the house which was now surrounded by bale walls, ready to suck up the moisture if we hadn't swept it away. When we arrived at the Trading Post we were met by the usual crew that included Dan Bond, Max Valdez, Obed, Lorraine, Jerry, the owner and his son and daughter who also worked there. They were all getting used to our regular visits and it was a jovial, gregarious gathering. Dan said to the others that he thought I was the image of an old time gun slinger. I protested that I didn't even know how to sling a gun! Dan explained the source of his inspiration, saying that he thought my name sounded like it should have come out of a Zane Grey novel. Perhaps that false impression was aided by my dirty Levis, bad shave and battered ten gallon straw hat...and my obvious western accent!

The little group at the Trading Post was a good sample of the demographics of the San Luis Valley many of whom trace their ancestry to the pioneers who came to the valley in the mid to late 1800s. Some were the descendants of *Hispano* farmers and ranchers from the villages of northern New Mexico. Max Valdez, the father of our straw bale provider, Lionel Valdez, was one of these. His grandfather came from the Española area over 100 years before to establish the farm in Capulín now operated by Lionel. Others came from Utah as part of the large Mormon migration, early in the era of settlement. Jerry, the Trading Post owner, was also the local Mormon Bishop. Others, mostly Anglos, came from eastern America, especially during the Colorado population explosion after the Civil War.

THURSDAY, AUGUST 10

This was a special day. We put the last bale into the house at about 1:45 this afternoon. Chris had the honor with Brian's help. The vertical dimension of the bale and all others in the top course had been meticulously reduced by Brian using a chain saw.

Soon after the last bale had been placed we had a good rain so we wrapped things up, literally, with our many tarps. We now have enough of them to cover a city block, if there were one around. Tomorrow the roof is due to arrive from La Jara, so it won't be a work day. We think the house is looking very good. We like the window and door placement and are anxious to get the roof on so that rain protection becomes easier. In other news, the cows are trying to come down out of the forest, prematurely by about a month, to feed on and trample the inviting meadow grass. That's a clear "no-no" since the cutting and baling won't be completed for another week or two or three, depending on the whim of the farmer.

August 10. The final bale.

During the next ten days or so we were occupied with the roof. The joists were manufactured in Albuquerque and delivered by the Trading Post. They were big unwieldy wooden triangles. We thought it would speed up the installation process if we hung them upside down inside the house, resting them on the north and south perimeter beams. Wrong! The weight and horizontal pressure on the beams caused them to bend outwards. When we discovered the problem we quickly remove the joists and used a "come along" to pull the beams back into alignment. Fortunately, no permanent damage was done. During this period of time we had frequent rain delays that interrupted our work and made us race to drape the walls with our tarps. There were often big puddles left that we swept down an interior drain.

TUESDAY, AUGUST 16

We had kind of a late start today. Actually, I was there early but Baudelio and Brian arrived at 10:00 and 11:00 respectively. That's okay. There was quite a bit of rain water to sweep up and Tarps to take down to get ready for work. Part of the roof is up and we have our system organized so that work tomorrow will go well.

Brian was late in part because he was thrown by one of Baudelio's horses on Saturday. It reared up and tossed him on his back on pretty hard ground. Unfortunately he was carrying a rifle strapped to his back which he fell on. Lucky he wasn't severely injured.

On the way to town this morning I passed our neighbor the cowboy, out for a ride with his cute daughter. I also passed dozens of horses and colts, the next generation of *Hispano* horses. It's a powerful tradition among northern New Mexico and southern Colorado *Hispano*s to have horses. You don't necessarily see them being ridden very often but it is important to have them and the colts are lovely to look at this time of year.

Wafer board sheathing. Note neglected overhang on right edge.

By the end of that week we had finished the rough roof. As the picture indicates, the pattern was to put up five joists at a time and then cover them with wafer board sheathing. It took a lot of lifting and some inventive adjustments to keep the joist peaks on line.

On the morning after we had "finished" the roof, Baudelio noticed a significant error we had made. We had failed to provide an overhang on the west end of the roof, a dumb oversight and difficult to remedy with eight foot wide plywood pieces firmly attached to the joists. The mistake is clearly visible in the above photo. The question of how to fix it spoiled my sleep but sometime in the middle of the night a solution occurred to me. We would cut off the outside edge of the sheathing, from the lower edge to the peak and all the way down the other side of the roof, a very long cut with a skill saw. Then we would replace those outside pieces with new ones that would extend fifteen inches out over the gable. It worked and we moved on.

We had heard from our plumber and electrician that he would be ready to come up to the valley the following Sunday morning to give us power and water to the work site. He gave me a shopping list while we were in Santa Fe where we could shop for the materials and supplies needed for both jobs. We loaded up the truck on Saturday evening. Carl was a notorious early riser and hard worker so I was up at 4:45 on Sunday morning and headed north. Carl and I linked up near Tres Piedras and arrived at the work site together at about 8:00. There had been heavy rain and things were wet and muddy in the valley.

As previously mentioned, the well and our new power pole were next to the old cabin, about 100 yards from the new place. The trench had been dug that would carry both water and electric lines from the old place to the new one. We started work at 8:30 and with a few scary hitches, like possible missing parts, the water and power lines were installed by noon. After Carl had unconnected the PVC pipes to the old cabin, we discovered that our can of PVC glue was over the hill and without glue we couldn't put things back together again. That would leave us without water at both the building site and the old cabin where we were living.

As I may have mentioned, Santa Rita provides miracles when there is a real crisis, although in less serious cases she only puts us to a lot of work and worry. In this case we really needed supernatural assistance. I drove up the canyon to our neighbor Don Van Soelen's cabin in the forlorn hope that he would have the vital glue. Would you believe it? He did! He had a tiny can of cement, just brought up the day before for a small plumbing job. It was just enough for us to get the job done. So we now have water to our job site hydrant and power to a temporary receptacle which will allow us to work independently, without reliance on the facilities at the old cabin. We could now put away over one hundred yards of extension cords. Hurray!

The next week was a period of transition. We covered the east and west gables with wafer board, a version of plywood. The result was a house that was completely enclosed except for windows and the one doorway. It was satisfying to see such tangible results. No more sweeping rain water down the drain and the bales were now protected against the rain. The hundreds of dollars in tarps were now stacked casually inside the house and would probably never be needed on the job again. It began to look more like a house every day.

What a marvel. I thought that our sense of accomplishment must be close to what Robert Oppenheimer must have felt when the bomb went off near White Sands about fifty years earlier, except what we were doing was so much more constructive. I thought of Oppenheimer because I had met him in 1951 beside a swimming pool in Princeton, New Jersey, where he had retreated to the Institute of Advanced Study at Princeton University after having his loyalty questioned by Senator Joseph McCarthy and others. Since I'm already on a tangent I should mention that I also met his mentor, Albert Einstein, that summer in Princeton, one of the memorable experiences of my life. I was the house guest of my girlfriend's parents. Her mother was a concert pianist and on a couple of occasions Einstein brought his fiddle to their house to play duets. My friend and I were the audience, listening raptly from the next room. What an experience! This ramble started with my thoughts about what a wonderful, tangible sense of accomplishment it was to build a house, so much more satisfying an achievement than creating an atomic bomb or even delivering the most transcendent memorandum of my business career.

As I was thinking these great thoughts after work with Baudelio one evening, enjoying our second beers, I noticed green sprouts pushing up through the waste straw we had distributed on the disturbed soil around the cabin. Baudelio took a closer look and said, "That's oats." So our straw was not entirely sterile and we were restoring the disturbed landscape with one of the major crops of the San Luis Valley, another fringe benefit of building with straw bales.

Baudelio and I had put on the roofing paper and the rain protection was now even more complete. Even though we still needed to complete the roof with metal pro panel sheets, we were looking ahead to the plastering job. It seemed likely that Baudelio would be too occupied with his hay harvest to help with plastering so we were in the market for another contractor. On the way to town one afternoon we stopped at an unusual two story adobe house on the short cut to the Chama highway. It was being upgraded and we stopped to admire the plaster job. We learned that the contractor was Michael Raél who lived in Florida (that's Flo-RÍ-Da), Colorado. We thought we might check him out. At the Trading Post we put in the final order for the pro-panel metal roof and fittings, chicken wire to wrap the bale walls, flues and triple wall pipe for the stoves and other assorted materials. Dan Bond and the other Trading Post regulars had nice things to say about Michael Raél but also recommended Fernando Cruz who lived in Antonito. Baudelio didn't know him but thought he might be a "wetback." He thought that would be a good thing because he would probably be a hard worker, highly motivated and inexpensive. Baudelio wanted to check out Cruz before calling Mike Raél. So we let the San Luis Valley system work its way.

In the meantime, the windows and front door were due to arrive the following week. While we were at the Trading Post we also bought fifty pounds of 8 penny nails, two gable vents, eighty joist hangers for the porch and other needed things. Dan Bond also gave me the short version of "Roof 101" so we would be ready for that exciting chapter. Back at the new cabin, with walls and roof enclosing the whole building, the interior was all one big room, waiting to be subdivided into smaller spaces.

One big room. No interior weight bearing walls.

Morning temperatures were consistently around 48 degrees and a fire in the old cabin stove felt good. The chamisas were in full bloom as were many other fall flowers. It was definitely late summer. In Mogote, La Jara and Antonito, everyone was gearing up for the end of the hay harvest. More and more pickup trucks stacked high with firewood (*leña*) were seen on the road out of the National Forest. As busy as we were we didn't forget to remember why we were there. Looking out the east window of the old cabin with the muted colors of a threatening sky … distant thunder… I could see a thousand shades of green in our dry country and as many shapes as you can imagine up to the horizon that slanted sharply to the right… a few ponderosas, and lots of cedars and junipers vividly etched against the grey sky. The next few days produced only modest progress. Baudelio was engaged in his main occupation of farming, but we did make a start on the porch which would extend all across the front of the building. Brian operated Baudelio's John Deere front end loader to prepare the slope of the yard for that job.

Getting ready for the porch.

During the frequent afternoon rains, Chris, Brian and I laid out most of the interior wall locations, marking them with chalk lines. One of the great things about this kind of construction is that you can review and modify decisions about interior dimensions because there are no interior load-bearing walls. The only real restraints are the plumbing features imbedded in the slab. We modified the shape and size of a couple of bedrooms and our one closet.

It had been kind of a strange week with lots of rain and mostly cloudy skies. The main issue frustrating us was ambiguity in the drawings for the porch and its roof. We had to fall back on our creativity and inventiveness. The first question was how to attach the porch foundation to the house foundation. Our first try, a header bolted to the foundation, failed because we couldn't penetrate the foundation with our drill bits. On Friday evening as we were preparing for dinner, Baudelio and Brian stopped by with a new idea: why not lay a line of railroad ties along the front foundation of the house to support the floor joists for the deck? It made eminent good sense and we agreed to go to La Jara to buy ties the next morning.

SATURDAY, AUGUST 26

We borrowed Baudelio's pickup and headed for the Trading Post where we bought the six railroad ties we needed. The ties were so long that we couldn't close the tail gate but they were so heavy as to be almost immobile. On the way back we stopped at the drugstore in Antonito to buy a newspaper. Shortly after we pulled away from the curb we noticed a man running behind us and frantically waving his arms and pointing back at the drugstore. I was mystified and looked back over my shoulder to see what might be wrong. To my surprise and chagrin it appeared we were down to four railroad ties. We turned around and thanked the man who had chased us half way through Antonito. He said, "Your ties are in front of the drugstore!" Sure enough, they were right at the curb where we had deposited them when we pulled out. We made our way more cautiously home with the full load after Chris and I reloaded the heavy ties.

One day Brian returned from a midday trip to Antonito and excitedly reported the dramatic news that on the way up the high road he spotted an animal which on closer inspection through the telescopic sight on his high powered rifle turned out to be a "timber wolf." Baudelio and I were politely but distinctly surprised since no wolves have been sighted in New Mexico for several decades. But we were pleased by his discovery. That night while having dinner with us after chasing cows back into the forest, Baudelio agreed with a big smile and a happy chuckle that Brian had almost certainly seen a good sized coyote. The animal probably owed his or her life to the misidentification, since Brian probably would have killed the wolf if he had known it was a coyote!

The reader will have noticed frequent references to animals in these pages. They were always with us; elk, deer, beavers often, cows almost all of the time, and occasionally a more exotic porcupine, lesser weasel, or mountain lion, not to mention dozens upon dozens of birds. Our life list of Los Pinos birds contains over a hundred species. But the two animals at the top of the food chain are clearly the mountain lion and the black bear. The lions are more discrete and nocturnal and we seldom see them. Fortunately their diet doesn't seem to include Baudelio's cattle very often.

The bears we seem to see a bit more often although they too don't make a habit of appearing during the daylight hours very often. During the drier summers we see them more often. They are ravenously hungry and their diet is opportunistic. They will eat almost anything. One summer evening as Baudelio and Arlene were having supper in their cabin kitchen just down the road from us, they heard a disturbance just outside their screen door. When they investigated they discovered a large black bear sitting in the seat of their pickup truck munching away on a bag of frito chips they had left there with the truck's windows down. When he had finished his first course he came over to rattle the screen door and ask for further handouts. They told him to get lost and he wandered off although he was seen assessing the neighborhood cuisine for the next several days.

A few years ago our upstream neighbor, Jimmy Van Soelen, found that one of Baudelio's cows had died, apparently of natural causes, and the carcass was in a ditch not far from his front door. During the next week while more or less fresh meat was available, Jimmy identified as many as five different bears enjoying the buffet style banquet. They ranged in size from a big old male down to two young ones. The younger and smaller bears showed great deference for the old guy and faded off into the woods whenever he appeared. Jimmy is an accomplished wildlife photographer and the bears were willing or at least unconcerned subjects. They were close enough for him to take studio quality portraits of each individual and the whole group. He observed them so closely and so often that he noted individual markings and demeanor. He came to know them so well that he gave them names. Jimmy said that the big male was one of the most handsome black bears he had ever seen so he was called "Handsome." Another had a distinctive white patch on his chest and he was called "Key Hole." Then there was a matching pair that looked like two year olds that he named "The Twins." When the feast was finally gone the bears disappeared, leaving only a few scraps for the coyotes, turkey vultures, magpies and ravens. I'm sure most of the valley neighbors have their own bear stories and probably a few mountain lion stories too.

Meanwhile, back at the construction project, with the railroad ties in hand we were ready to tackle the porch. The deck was supported on the house side by the ties placed on the ground next to the foundation and on the outer edge by six heavy concrete piers that had been poured by our cement contractor.

The working drawings for the porch were ambiguous, so we proceeded with our own handmade design and the work went along quite well. The result was a sturdy deck and six posts that would support the roof. The drawings also failed to show us how to attach the roof joists to the house but we worked that out too, proving once again that common sense beats inferior professional design every time.

Porch foundation challenges.

Late August. Porch roof joists going up.

One day as we enjoyed a late afternoon beer, sitting on the new porch frame we watched a good sized coyote walking the field that Baudelio had just cut today. Brian always saw coyotes as potential prey. We appreciated them as clever survivors who ate mice and other critters. After we enjoyed our beers we watched Brian head up the canyon and a few minutes later we heard a fusillade of rifle shots indicating either that Brian's trophy coyote was avoiding his shots or was as full of holes as Swiss cheese. I was sure we would find out which it was when he arrived the next morning. Sure enough, it was reported to be "target practice." By this time in late summer we all hoped the monsoon would end soon. Things were a little too green and wet and the river was high and muddy every day. Work was often interrupted and the mosquitoes came out in force whenever it rained. The good news was that Chris brought up and we roasted the first green chile of the 1995 crop.

The next day after another trip to La Jara, we came home on the low road and finally met Mr. Cruz who was doing plaster work on the little church in the Colorado village of San Antonio. As suspected, he was from Mexico and spoke little English, but our mixed English and Spanish conversation led us to believe that he might be the right man for our job. We still had our work cut out for us to get ready for him; chicken wire, metal lathe and dressing the bales.

The little villages on both sides of the state line were settled in the second half of the 1800s. Some of them, like Ortiz, Colorado and Los Pinos, New Mexico had substantial populations in their hay day. Ortiz is reported to have had as many as 500 people at its peak. Some places still survive with a handful of people. Others have completely disappeared. Some, like San Antonio and San Miguel still have their well cared for and beloved little churches, but the people are mostly gone. Often the village names persist and are still used by local people to identify the places where people used to live in greater numbers.

Outside and Inside

At the beginning of September, we were about three months into the project and things were looking quite impressive. We had made real strides towards completing the porch from hell. The roof joists were up and we were ready to put on the sheathing and roofing felt. Our wonderful pro-panel roof had been delivered along with six windows and three interior doors. We were now looking forward with curiosity and the usual uncertainty to the next challenges: installing the metal roof, shingling under the gables and finally beginning to think seriously about the inside of the house. In the meantime, Baudelio had some of the hay cut and baled and we were looking forward to his availability to work on our project.

Chris and I had decided that we couldn't go on without our own pickup truck. There were just too many chores that required us to borrow Baudelio's truck. So on one of our weekends in Santa Fe we went out and bought our very own Toyota Tacoma. One of its first missions was to make its maiden journey to the La Jara Trading Post to collect about

500 pounds of Irish wood stove, purchased from our traditional hardware store in the Amish country of Ohio. The stove was fork lifted onto the bed of our truck in its shipping crate and we were off to Santa Rita. We unpacked it and removed all of its moving parts to lighten the load but it was still too heavy for us to carry. So we scooted it off the truck, across the deck and into the house on 2 X 8 skids. We still faced the hurdle of how to raise it up to install the legs but we had theories about how to make that happen.

The next day we thought we would start the metal roof installation but as we were about to climb onto the roof there was a totally unexpected clap of thunder and it started to rain lightly. So instead we installed the six windows without any major misadventures. They looked great and made the building look even more like a house.

The house now has windows.

Since the weather wasn't cooperating that afternoon, Chris and I drove to La Jara to shop and get one more bit of roof instruction from Dan Bond. The two big issues on our critical path at that stage were getting the roof done and getting a firm commitment on the exterior plaster job. When those priorities were ironed out we could address the interior walls and the ceiling structures that had to be handled, more or less, before we could make progress on the plumbing and electrical work. At about this time our hopes of getting Baudelio's undivided attention suffered a setback. His wife, Arlene, had an automobile accident that nearly totaled her car and left her pretty badly banged up.

The two of them were real partners in their marriage and in their shared work, especially in the harvest season. They were both small in stature but large in their capacity for physical work. Baudelio was strong as a bull after a lifetime of every day outdoor work. Arlene was tiny, barely five feet tall and weighing not more than one hundred pounds, but she had worked as a truck driver in her youth before earning her teaching credentials at Adams State College in Alamosa. During the hay season they were both needed in the field. She drove the big, clumsy old flatbed truck with a mechanical bale loader while he built the load. Then the two of them drove the precarious load up the high road and down the other side to Mogote, where the bales were stacked to provide winter feed for their cattle.

They were the last survivors of the generations of *Hispano* pioneers who homesteaded Santa Rita in the late nineteenth and early twentieth centuries. Baudelio was the grandson of one homesteader, Hipolito Garcia and perhaps the great grandson of another, Juan Bautista Gallegos. Arlene told us that her father, a Martinez, was a "red Indian." When pressed to provide further definition of his heritage, she was unable to do so. He could have had Ute blood since they were the last dominant tribe in the San Luis Valley, or he might have been Navajo. What may be more likely is that he was part of the ubiquitous group of people called *genízaros*, people of mixed blood or detribalized Indians, captured by both *Hispano*s and nomadic Indians during the hostilities that were common during much of the Spanish and Mexican eras. These people were bought and sold by their captors and often were incorporated into *Hispano* families throughout the region. Arlene's facial features could easily be seen as identifying her as one who came from such lineage. In later years the impression was even stronger. As people age, I think their faces more clearly reveal their history When asked where her people came from, Arlene's answer was, "We've always been here." In a sense, knowing what we know and not knowing the full truth, she may have been right about that.

In any event, her injuries made it impossible for her to help so we quickly agreed that Brian and I would pitch in whenever Baudelio returned from Mogote with an empty truck. I would drive the truck and Brian would help Baudelio build the load. Proceeding in that fashion, the day finally arrived when we would tackle the metal roof after weeks of agonizing. It didn't get off to the smoothest start.

THURSDAY, SEPTEMBER 7

God damn rain! It cut Baudelio and me off at about 2:00 when we were about done with the backside and we almost had our first bad accident. There was thunder in the area and I said, "Baudelio, we need to get off of here." He said, "Let's just finish these last two panels." Then it started to rain gently. He was well up on the roof and I was on top of the extension ladder, holding the bottom of the panel that ran from the eaves to the peak, about seventeen feet long. I said, "Baudelio, it's going to get slippery." He said, "We'll just finish this one." Then he slipped and skidded slowly down the roof towards me. I was well braced and tried to slow his slide. Not possible. We tangled; he toppled and fell to the ground on his back, a ten foot fall. My ladder tipped and I fell in the other direction. He just missed some big rocks and popped back up, unhurt, as did I. As soon as we confirmed our good health, my first words were, "I hope Chris didn't see that." She did. When she got closer she said, "What's going on here?" I responded, "We heard thunder and decided it was time to come down." Baudelio added, "We came down the fast way." That was enough roof for today. Besides, it's been raining ever since. Fucking rain!

Dangerous roof installation on a rainy day.

Early the next week we finished the main roof panels and installed the ridge cap and edge strips at the lower end of the roof without further incident. We were really glad to get off the roof. The Monday weather was mixed, with rain and wind in the afternoon but it cleared up and we had a beautiful clear evening. We listened to Hank Williams songs during dinner in the old cabin next to a hot stove. After working on the roof for a few days I guess we and Hank Williams were "ready to meet the Angel of death."

With the roof job behind us we were ready for another transition. This time it was preparing for stucco, closing up any remaining cracks and fissures and getting things in shape for the more detailed interior work such as putting up the ceilings, framing the walls and installing the stove. By this time the cows knew it was really fall. They were all down with us by this time, both Baudelio's and lots of strangers who had drifted in from the other side of the Cruces Basin Wilderness. We chased them away several times but they responded reluctantly and patiently, knowing we were a passing phenomenon that they had to put up with this time of year. It would all sort itself out in a few weeks when cows and owners would be reunited but until then we were all part of the commons, which was not all bad. It gave us a sense of community, in a sort of involuntary way, which, after all, is the normal way in most communities. Another fall phenomenon was the sudden disappearance of the mosquitoes. They were virulent one week and completely gone the next.

WEDNESDAY, SEPTEMBER 20

It's getting to be autumn with cooler nights and mostly sunny days. The pace in Santa Rita and in our larger neighborhood, the San Luis Valley, is frenetic as the harvest concludes and winter approaches, giving everyone a sense of urgency. This is definitely a place where the physical world intrudes into the lives of people and nature's seasonal changes are more than just fuel for conversation. Baudelio has been out of the link for about two weeks. He finished the bale pick up in Santa Rita yesterday—about 2,000 bales—more than last year despite not cutting as much acreage. It's a tribute to his ingenuity that the old equipment made it through another year.

The valley is full of cows—must have been fifty across the river today when Chris and I went across to cut fire wood. Baudelio had been curious about his missing big red bull, still unaccounted for until this afternoon when he was discovered with a harem of cows up in the Lobo Creek area. Baudelio was much relieved.

He had lost a valuable bull last year for unknown reasons. Brian thinks it was aliens. The house progresses in fits and starts but in an entirely satisfactory way. We continue with mostly readying the outside for stuccoing, stuffing straw into openings at the top of the walls and installing wire mesh. The plaster crew is still expected at the beginning of October. Yesterday we completed the installation of the wonderful Waterford Stanley kitchen stove and today we completed the flue and stove pipe work through the roof. We still haven't had our ceremonial first fire, but we're looking forward to that.

Time for some indoor work.

The next day we went to work on the frame interior walls. I drove to Alamosa to rent a "nailer," which will allow us to drive nails through the 2 X 4 and 2 X 6 inch plates and into the concrete floor. The nailer is in effect a gun that fires a blank 22 caliber cartridge, driving the nail through the board and into the floor. This was Brian's kind of work; indoor gun powder! That afternoon we made a mysterious discovery. An exterior wall that we had just been working on was seen to be almost broken through from the outside. One bale was seriously displaced inward by some unidentified exterior force. The outside of the bale was significantly torn up by the event; not serious in terms of the integrity of the wall but still quite baffling. Could it have been a cow with head worms, a bear, an elk scraping his antlers or perhaps, Brian thought, an alien? Who knows? And we never found an answer.

A chimney for our wood cook stove.

We began to have the satisfying feeling that we were quite far along and that as the season was winding down, so was our project. The work we were doing was preparing us for Carl Lindahl's visit at the end of the month to install the electrical circuits and size up the remaining plumbing work. We had the shower stall on site and the water heater was available at the Trading Post. The house was closed up. We had installed the front door the previous week. Soon we would have electricity and water inside and be able to camp out in the place. The long awaited plaster job was important in many ways, not least because it would exclude the rest of the Los Pinos food chain and give us some degree of privacy from those four legged neighbors, including the mysterious wall buster, who we wanted to exclude from our indoor space.

The interior wall frames are essentially complete after a good long day of work and we had a better sense of how we would live there. It was pretty chilly in the morning. It was below freezing and snowed a bit and rained during part of the morning. We worked hard, had green chile stew for lunch and finished at about 6:00. It felt like we would have a hard freeze that night but I took an outdoor shower at about 6:45 that was very invigorating. Baudelio stopped in the evening and for the second day in a row suggested that if the Cruz party didn't show up he would be glad to do the plastering. That would have to be sorted soon and if Baudelio took on the job we would all have to be involved. That seemed to be a good solution that would eliminate any uncertainty about how and when the work would be done. Baudelio had access to a small electric mixer we could use and it would be good to not have to deal with a contractor. We had a truly spectacular sunset and by 7:00 it was pitch dark.

At the end of that week my son Mason and I had a lovely little adventure and detour on our way to Santa Fe. We took the low road down along the river to San Miguel. Instead of continuing on down to Highway 285, we turned south at San Miguel and crossed the river on a Forest Service road that led us past the back side of San Antonio Mountain and then east on another Forest road to Lagunitas, a magical place of linked beaver ponds, small bodies of water which, as their name suggests, were the Lagunitas. Then we were faced with the choice of making our way back about 25 miles east to route 285 or taking the rustic road less traveled to the west. We chose the unknown western option. Our U.S.G.S maps suggested that it might be possible to make our way through along the southern edge of the Cruces Basin Wilderness and come out on the other side near Cumbres Pass, all on what was described on our maps as Forest Road 87. This choice gave us a three hour long drive on a very primitive four wheel drive trail, rising to an elevation of about 11,000 feet. The only people we saw, except for a solitary fisherman at Lagunitas, were two Forest Service workers who we met at the darkest and deepest woods we passed through. They assured us that it was possible to get through. The journey took us above tree line and gave us a spectacular view north over the Cruces Basin to Los Pinos Canyon above the Toltec Gorge. We finally came out of the wilderness onto Highway 17 just one mile north of Cumbres Pass. The trip provided one of the grandest, emptiest scenes we had ever seen in New Mexico or anywhere else for that matter.

After reaching the paved road we proceeded south to Chama and on back to Santa Fe for a city weekend that included a welcome restaurant dinner and a visit to the Farmers Market. We also did the shopping for electrical supplies for Carl Lindahl's planned visit to the cabin the following weekend.

The Ute Indians

In describing the trip my son and I made through the high country of the southern San Juan Mountains, I called it a grand and empty scene. It was certainly grand but it was not empty. It was full of an amazing diversity of animals, birds and plant life that thrive in that broad, well watered wilderness. What made it seem empty, in a way, was the absence of people. That had not always been the case. It had long been used by the various native peoples, who contested this vast region. But during the early historic period and the late prehistoric period it had been part of the Ute homeland.

People only recently came up with the new concept of wilderness. In earlier times the American wilderness was the huge unexplored part of our continent that was not yet occupied and used by the new people who came mostly from Europe to conquer the new world. But even then the wilderness was occupied and used by its native peoples. To those people the places where they lived were their homelands and had been forever, according to their origin stories. Their population density was low by contemporary measures but they occupied and exercised dominion over their territory.

In the twentieth century, after European Americans had dispossessed the native inhabitants of their historic homelands all across the continent, what remained of the original pristine wild places had been dramatically diminished. In both economic and aesthetic terms, scarcity drives up price and value. People began to treasure the shrinking supply of relatively undisturbed land and responded by creating what came to be known as the wilderness movement to preserve these precious remnants from the encroachment and impact of man's presence. These special places were to be protected in their existing condition and man was to be only an occasional and unobtrusive visitor. The irony of this development must have been apparent to contemporary members of the ancient Indian tribes, including the Utes, whose ancestral domain was being put to a new use by the invaders.

An engaging story of the Ute Tribe was written by Fred A. Conetah, a member of the tribe, in his book, *A History of the Northern Ute People*. He described how the people came to occupy a huge territory that included areas that became parts of Utah, Colorado, New Mexico and Wyoming. These people were loosely organized into family-based groups living in separate but adjoining areas. They had a strong sense of their shared culture, spoke the same language and came together frequently for trade, social interchange and marriage. They often participated together in ceremonial and religious practices. Fred Conetah described an original homeland of about 225,000 square miles, extending as for south as Abiquiu, New Mexico. They were semi nomadic, living mostly in the mountains in the summer and returning to habitual valley and desert areas in the winter. The larger groupings were called bands. Those who inhabited the area that is today's Conejos County, Colorado and northern Rio Arriba County, New Mexico were the Moache, Kopota, Weemanuche and Taviwach bands. The places where they hunted, gathered and fished were expanded immensely when they began to acquire horses from the Spanish by trade and capture during the frequent raids on New Mexico settlements. They were active traders and began to use corn, squash, beans and other products provided by the Pueblo People. Both the Kopota and the Moache bands used the region encompassing Santa Rita as part of their hunting and fishing range and as their defensive fortress during times of conflict with other tribes.

These two bands were served during Territorial days by Indian Agents headquartered in Taos and Cimarron, New Mexico. One of these Agents was Kit Carson. Another was one of the founders of Guadalupe, later Conejos, whose name was Lafayette Head. Both of these men married *Hispano* women and were assimilated into the majority *Hispano* community. In early census records Carson was identified as Cristobal Carson and in Conejos Parish records, Head was listed as "Rafael Cabezón," *cabezón* being the Spanish word for big head. I know it sounds like a bilingual joke, but it's not!

Back in Santa Rita Canyon, where we were building our cabin, the only faint traces of the long presence of the Utes are the arrow heads frequently found on the banks of the Rio de Los Pinos where the Indians hunted and fished when the place was in the heart of their homeland. Again, ironically, they left little to mark their long presence in this new American style wilderness, unlike those who came after they were gone and changed its appearance significantly.

After our relaxing weekend in Santa Fe we were back at work. In the last week of September, we finished framing the inside walls.

Framing the interior walls.

Chicken wire stucco netting before plastering.

Then we moved on to work at wrapping the building with stucco netting, and stuffing straw into voids here and there. We also did some general neatening up on the perimeter of the project. The composting toilet was on site but would not be installed until later. Our wood cook stove and its flue were ready for the first ceremonial fire but we hadn't found time for that event. Brian reported that the first New Mexico deer hunting season was about to open, so we could expect to see hunters setting up their camps in the neighborhood. The seasons were changing and we could see the fall colors in the aspen groves and the river edge cottonwoods.

WEDNESDAY, OCTOBER 4

Well, the journal and our frame of mind have suffered a major setback. Last Thursday morning Chris tried to use a small table to reach and clean the top of the refrigerator in the old cabin. It collapsed under her weight and she fell and broke four bones in her left foot. After struggling to get her into the truck we drove to the Conejos County Hospital in La Jara where Dr. Celada confirmed the break. He recommended that we take her to Santa Fe where more sophisticated care was available. Early the next morning we saw Dr. Jan Bear who confirmed the diagnosis and rigged her with a soft cast. Beyond that it was simply a matter of taking the time necessary for the break to heal while keeping her weight off the foot. We rented crutches and Chris gamely agreed to come back to the mountains that weekend so we could keep our appointment with Carl Lindahl. This is not a good place for crutches and needless to say Chris and I are depressed and disappointed that this injury will deprive us of the fun of working together through the next steps leading to moving into the cabin.

When we were building the cabin together, Chris had been my wife and partner for 39 years. At this writing we've been together for 59 years. Her injury and partial incapacity reminded me once again how much I relied on her support. We had had a happy and satisfying life together but it had not been without challenges and setbacks which we survived in part because of her toughness, tenacity and wisdom. Her down to earth common sense often provided answers that with my more analytical approach I couldn't see. I worried about the big issues but she brought me back to reality by telling me, "It was worse when we were younger and you didn't even know how to fry an egg." At any rate, whether it's fixing breakfast or fixing a financial challenge, it would have been a rough road without my small town banker's daughter, and she would be quick to remind me that both of her parents were small town bankers in two neighboring Indiana towns. On a more practical level, her injury was bad news for both of us. For her it was a pain in the foot; for me and the crew it was a pain in the ass! After that difficult weekend at the work site and a less than joyful first fire in the Waterford stove, we returned to Santa Fe. When I arrived at the work site on the following Monday without Chris, Baudelio and Brian were preparing to start the plaster job the next day. Baudelio was an experienced plasterer but had obviously never tried to apply it to a straw wall and was skeptical about the outcome. Nevertheless, it went quite smoothly as I tried to keep up with them, cranking out the mud in the little electric mixer. We were sloppy but the results were good. Our little mixer worked fine.

The little mixer that could.

We had been enjoying comfortable Indian summer weather for some time but now that we were working outside it suddenly turned cold and windy. We even had a little snow. So we shut down and moved inside, started a fire and did some final plaster preparation on the inside walls. During his visit the previous weekend, Carl Lindahl had done much of the interior electrical wiring that had to be installed before the walls and ceilings were completed. Wires that traversed the walls were simply stuffed into the horizontal crack between bales and the boxes were attached to vertical posts or framed walls.

THURSDAY, OCTOBER 5

It was a beautiful but cold sixteen degrees early this morning. We worked on the rest of the stucco netting outside. It was just too cold to work with plaster outside until afternoon. Brian went to town at noon with his pay check and never came back, so Baudelio and I did a bit of plastering until 4:00 when we decided it was too cold to continue. Still, we're in pretty good shape. We're done with the nasty job of preparing all the exterior walls for plaster. That job involved sewing the chicken wire onto the bales. From the outside, one guy pushes the bale needle through a bale with rebar wire hooked through the hole in the point. Then the guy on the inside takes the wire out of the needle. The guy on the outside pulls the needle out, pushes it through another bale and the guy on the inside attaches the wire to the needle that is then pulled out, bringing with it the wire that can then be tied across to where the wire was originally inserted. It makes a nice tight connection between the chicken wire and bale so that it will support the plaster.

With a little luck it will be warmer tomorrow and we can make good time before the weekend. The day was beautiful, crisp and clear but very chilly. I had a fire going in the new house at 8:00 and it stayed nice and warm. In the real world O.J. Simpson was declared innocent by the L.A. jury, the Cleveland Browns lost on Monday night football to Buffalo and the Cleveland Indians won their first post season game in 50 years, beating the Boston Red Socks 5 to 4 in 13 innings. The Serbs, Muslims and Croats of Bosnia are threatening to declare peace. Obviously I went to town and bought a Denver Post.

The next day was typical for the season. The morning temperature was 10 degrees but it turned out to be a gorgeous day with the afternoon temperature at about 55 degrees. We made substantial progress with the plaster. In the afternoon I took my chain saw up the high road and blocked up a nice aspen we had been coveting all summer and another one that had been blown down by big winds a few days earlier. Then back to Santa Fe to check on Chris who was being brave but bored in her handicapped state. We found time for my first real haircut since the project began and made a quick drive to Albuquerque on the weekend to buy beds and other furniture for the new place.

By late in the next week we had almost finished the second exterior coat of plaster and the house was beginning to look like a traditional northern New Mexico adobe with walls that were undulating and uneven but very pleasing to the eye. Baudelio lavished his praise on the work with the succinct comment, "It's pretty."

Exterior Stucco Complete.

The weather moderated to accommodate our work with warm and sunny days and night temperatures just below freezing. One evening as Baudelio and I were savoring an end of the day beer, he pointed out a coyote in among the cows down by the corral. The cows and their rapidly growing calves either ignored the coyote or occasionally charged him in a gentle way to let him know that his company was tolerated but not welcome. It was now the middle of October and we had just finished the second coat of exterior stucco. The recipe for our mix, in shovels, was 2 masonry cement, 1 regular Portland cement, 2 lime and 12 sand. We used a wet mix, lots of water, so the texture was quite thin. It clung nicely to the chicken wired bales and we could fill in the low spots by letting it set up a bit and then laying on more plaster. It also worked well, in terms of appearance, to rub the wall with rubber gloves after the plaster started to set up. The effect was to soften the finish and erase the tool marks. The middle of October was a wonderful time to be in Santa Rita. We had alternating Indian summer days and near winter days. Night time temperatures were trending rapidly down but the days were almost always good enough for outside work. The view up the valley was lovely as the trees began to change to their fall colors.

An October view up the canyon.

Most of the critical exterior work was finished enough to weather the winter. We planned to defer the final exterior stucco color coat until the next spring. There was still much to be done on the inside including walls, doors, bathroom and kitchen finish work and cabinets, ceilings, insulation above the ceilings and electrical and plumbing work. And we still faced the daunting and messy process of putting two coats of plaster on the inside of the exterior walls.

In preparation for plastering on the inside it was necessary to firmly attach the chicken wire to the bales. That was accomplished with the aid of adobe nails, eight inch long spiral nails with inch wide heads. We inserted the nails through the netting in a way that stretched it tightly against the bales. We stuffed loose straw into the nooks and crannies between the bales and adjoining structural materials. We also had to complete the rough carpentry wherever plaster would meet wood, including window sills and surrounds and door trim.

TUESDAY, OCTOBER 24

We've been so damn busy I haven't been able to record a couple of important passages. We've now moved out of the old cabin and into the new one; not the easiest transition but it's never easy to transform a construction project into a residence. The official inaugural was last Friday, Chris's first trip to the mountains for about three weeks. I drove down on Thursday to pick her up and we returned the next afternoon. We arrived at about 3:00. The place was filthy after a day of plastering and the house was cold. Brian and Baudelio had been working in the kitchen and living room area and everything was covered with plaster and dirt. We didn't even feel we could make our beds, which had to be assembled, until we cleaned up a bit. We had no option to staying in the new place because our partners were staying in the old cabin and Carl Lindahl was coming up early the next morning to do additional plumbing and electrical work. It was fairly overwhelming but we were not overwhelmed!

The event was softened and magnified by an invitation from Baudelio and Arlene. We were expected for dinner down the road at their cabin. We did the best we could with our cleanup work and drove down to their cabin. It was a great event, typically under planned with dinner served at about 9:30 to the exhausted guests. With Baudelio's encouragement we finished off the bottle of wine we had brought with us. They obviously thought this was a momentous occasion that called for a party, a good idea because if we had not been there we would have been frantically trying, with little effect, to put things in order in our place.

It was a warm and cordial evening like others we have come to treasure with the Garcias. We feel increasingly welcomed into their lives as friends and equals. It's a big part of why we love it here so much.

Carl arrived early on Saturday morning and worked like a Trojan until 8:00 in the evening when we took a break for a great dinner of flank steak, baked potatoes and trimmings all done on the new stove. We collapsed at about 10:00, were up at 7:00 and worked until noon when Carl left for Rio Rancho. By that time the wind was blowing a gale and we were having a blizzard. Progress! We had hot water in the kitchen sink which still didn't have a connected drain and we had a drain in the shower stall, which still didn't have running water. We also had our electric range hooked up and our refrigerator plugged in. And we had quite a few working lights, wall plugs and other conveniences.

In the two days since then we had started to turn the cabin into a home. It was relatively clean from time to time. The wood cook stove was working most of our waking hours and progress was being made on the interior finish, mostly plastered with at least one coat and two coats in a bed room and a critical kitchen wall where cabinets would be hung. We also had most of the ceiling and insulation up in the kitchen and living room area. That was a big job that has not been adequately reported here.

Ceiling panels going up. Twelve inches of insulation above ceiling.

Baudelio and Brian plastering bale walls.

It had been very cold and with ceiling insulation only partly installed we were unable to take full advantage of the great insulation value of our straw bale walls, but we were on our way. We were in the process of installing 12 inches of spun glass insulation above the ceilings that would have an insulation rating of R-38, so it would be cozy when it was done.

We hadn't had much help recently from Brian who was living out his fantasies as an elk hunter, unsuccessfully so far. We had a great visit one day from Baudelio's sister, Rose Trujillo, and her husband Victor who lived down the road in San Miguel. She was charming and as the official family historian had wonderful stories to tell about the old days in Santa Rita when she and her siblings were growing up in the senior Garcia house that we could see from our new place. Some of the older former residents of the valley had given up their affection for the old style houses but Rose loved and respected the traditional architecture and was obviously delighted that our place honored those traditions.

It had been rough sledding at times lately, not least because of Chris's broken foot. It was quite a scene one night at the Garcia's cabin with both women hobbling around on their crutches. But Chris and I agreed it was still good to be there. Chris, who was now driving again, went back to Santa Fe under her own power and I took one of my many trips to La Jara and worked with Baudelio on ceilings that afternoon. It was mild and sunny and a bit windy. The leaves were all down and we could clearly see the old *camposanto*, the family cemetery across the river, where some of the old homesteaders were buried. The cows were still drifting down out of the National Forest and enjoying the grass in the recently mowed meadows. It was warm and cozy in the cabin and one afternoon I cut and brought home a truck load of good mountain cottonwood made available by a blow down during a recent blizzard. The valley looked beautiful and was just about at rest for the winter.

As I look back on the summer of 1995 and my growing familiarity with Baudelio Garcia, and the tales of his grandparents and great grand-parents, I am struck by the similarities and differences in our stories. I am reminded that Baudelio and I share life spans that constitute a substantial fraction of the life span of our country. Like many Americans of our age, each of us is only two or three generations away from ancestors who lived on a frontier. Most of us who are now Americans came from immi-grant streams of the European diaspora that brought our families to these shores starting in the 1600s. Baudelio's European ancestors came from the Iberian Peninsula and mine from the British Isles. In both cases our grandfathers were born to pioneer settlers who came to live in two different border lands. Baudelio's grandfather and my grandfather were born in the 1860s, his to a family at the northern edge of the *Hispano* homeland of

New Mexico, mine to a Yankee family at the edge of the settled area of northern Maine.

The experiences of the two families must have had much in common in the beginning. They lived in houses that they built for themselves using the materials available in their homestead neighborhood. They were farmers and raised animals that contributed to their survival in harsh environments. We know from homestead records and the physical remnants of the original Santa Rita community that the settlers often built their first houses using the locally available timber. The most typical homestead cabin was made of notched logs. Others were constructed with adobe bricks fashioned at the building sites. Some, like our old cabin, were of *jacál* construction. It was common to lay vigas (beams) on the ground as a foundation for roughhewn wooden floors.

For a look at the home building practices on the eastern frontier at about the same time, I turn to a rustic autobiography my grandfather was cajoled into writing in his later years. He included a vivid description of a wilderness camp built by his father in the early 1870s that served as their home for much of the year.

> I must tell you about this camp. It was four rooms, built of round spruce logs notched at each end and laid very close to each other

with the bark on and chinked air tight with moss. It was one and a half stories high. The first floor was made of spruce logs hewn to one inch thickness and then adzed smooth. Each board was one half of a log. The first floor was divided into four rooms, living room, dining room and bedrooms. The insides of rooms were finished and paneled with spruce bark inside out which turned to a rich light brown. The panel strips were of small fir trees sawed through the center. The second floor was spruce boards brought up the river on row boats and was divided into four sleeping rooms. The roof was covered with three foot hand split cedar shingles and during a heavy rain we surely had lots of music. We also had another house for ice down by the pond. We cut these cakes of ice, put one or two on a sled and hauled them to the ice house until it was half full, then cover it with two or three feet of moss we gathered and it would keep all summer.

These regional precursors were surely good models for our own late twentieth century handmade cabin project. In fairness, we had many advantages including store bought manufactured materials, good water, electricity, internal combustion and electrically powered tools and modern transportation.

Despite the superficial similarities in the early lives of our two sets of pioneers, they were living at the edges of two very different cultures and communities. Baudelio's father was born into a world in which his culture, language and way of life would gradually be overwhelmed by new people coming from the east. My grandfather was born into a world in which his culture and language would dominate the future. The old world of Baudelio's father would shrink and decline in the course of his lifetime. My grandfather abandoned the pioneer life style of his father and merged into the unfamiliar new urban America. But, in his case, the new way grew out of his ethnic, cultural and linguistic traditions. Both Baudelio's father and my grandfather experienced dramatic dislocations from the old ways but the parallels were not symmetrical. In one, the transition was from the trailing edge of a culture and way of life that could be traced back for over a millennium, into a foreign and totally unfamiliar culture demanding a new set of skills and a new language. In my grandfather' situation, despite the novelty of his personal experiences, his life was in the continuum of his ancestors' culture, language and tradition.

TUESDAY, NOVEMBER 2

It's a miracle! We're much further along than we could have hoped for five months earlier. We're living in the cabin and it is getting more comfortable every day. This week has been productive with Baudelio and Brian both pitching in, Brian for his last week, "the last week of the best summer of my life", he said today. We had lunch with visiting friends in the middle of the plastering job, the second coat in the kitchen and living room. It looks great. Baudelio is a craftsman and the walls are beautiful.

Tomorrow we should see the last messy job finished as Baudelio and Brian complete the second coat of plaster in the back two bedrooms. Today I finished installing the insulation above the ceiling. Despite last night's snow and wind the temperature stayed above 70 degrees in the main room. It gets better every day as we tighten things up. Baudelio admitted yesterday that he had been insecure about undertaking the plastering job since he wasn't confident the stuff would stick to the straw and was afraid the plaster would crack. It's a wonderful job and much better than we would have gotten from a contractor.

We were about at the stage where Chris and I could putter on with the job without the daunting hurdles we faced all summer. It had taken us five months and we were now inside, warm, with electricity, hot and cold water, some places, about done with interior plaster walls and we had beds and other basic furniture. Getting the heavy floor to ceiling plywood wall board panels installed on the interior frame walls would be a big job but our time is cheap. We could continue to slowly move in, clean up, bring in more furniture, cooking implements and other necessities of life.

It was getting cold and the threat of serious snow increased every day but that was okay as long as we could stay there and keep it warm. What we had done was exciting, challenging and satisfying. Now it began to be more relaxing, less stressful and fun. We had a unique, beautiful, hand-made house that worked and blended nicely with the place.

TUESDAY, NOVEMBER 7

Lots of important milestones have come and gone, including paying off Brian last Friday. He's on his way to California and then back to Las Cruces for what he hopes is a new life. We finished the inside plaster on Monday (Baudelio's triumph). Chris and I are now on our own, moving on without help and living comfortably in our rough finished house. We came up from Santa Fe on Sunday, opened up (inside temperature 54 degrees) and prepared for Baudelio to arrive on Monday morning. He was right on time and we finished plastering by noon. I'm not sure whether he or we took the greatest satisfaction at reaching this critical check point. I'm sure he is glad to be done with every day deadlines and is ready to get back to the things that his life requires. We know that while much remains to be done, we are past the intensive construction phase.

It's wonderfully quiet here now. There are still a few hunters around but nobody is here in Santa Rita with us except for Baudelio and the wild animals. We had to make one of our trips to La Jara to get a piece of stove pipe to complete the installation of our second wood stove. It's done. Even without it, with the ceiling and insulation done we are snug as a bug in a rug. Cabin temperature was in the middle seventies during the day and around sixty in the morning when we got up to stoke the stove.

Next steps include moving on with putting up the interior wood panel walls and doors, finishing kitchen counters and getting ready for the final visit from our plumber friend. The wall panels are a big, heavy job that's taking lots of time. A place like this needs you and you need it, unlike a conventional residence that allows for passive occupancy. And if you don't have a whole lot of other obligations, which we don't, it's not a big burden. In fact, providing for one's own comfort can be a very satisfying way to spend time. It's a combination of short term chores, keeping up with wood cutting and house cleaning and staying ahead of long term needs like maintenance, repairs, and continuing the process of improving the place.

The big mistake, I think, is devoting too much capital to create a house that doesn't need you and makes the satisfying physical effort of daily life redundant. It helps a lot that this all takes place in a physical and cultural environment that is beautiful, comfortable, challenging and satisfying both aesthetically and emotionally.

Tomorrow we go to Santa Fe to take care of stuff; medical, financial, family responsibilities, planning, including fun things like a Thanksgiving trip to Minneapolis and a Christmas trip to Spain. These are among the other aspects of life that are important and may have helped bring us up here to this project and adventure in the wilds of northern New Mexico and southern Colorado.

Winding Down

My last journal entry for the year was on Wednesday, December 6, a quiet early winter day shared by Chris and me and the elk, deer and coyotes. Baudelio's cows and calves had made their annual trek over the northern ridge to their winter home in Mogote. The other part time human residents of Santa Rita had long since buttoned up their places for the winter, so we were alone in the valley. The work done the previous weekend with Carl Lindahl's help provided a perfect transition from the construction phase to everything that was to follow and would keep us busy well into the next year. That last Saturday with Carl we finished the remaining plumbing and electrical work. That evening after he left, Chris and I had our first hot showers in the completed shower stall. That was definitely a climactic event. The house worked like a charm; weather tight and cozy on a mild winter evening. Our two wood stoves practically ran us out of the house but we couldn't resist firing them up. All the overhead lights were installed, some of them by me under expert supervision. It would take time and effort to complete the job but the heavy lifting was behind us and we could begin to live in the cabin and get on with turning it into our second home.

As the year was winding down I often thought of Baudelio's indispensable help. I came to have a strong appreciation of the wholeness of his and Arlene's lives here in this scattered community on the edge of two states. In contrast to the more fragmented lives of late twentieth century Americans, he managed and executed all aspects of his job as a small scale farmer and rancher. His small cattle herd was the product of his planning and stewardship. He managed the land and the water that produced the hay that fed his cattle through the cycle of seasons and years. He operated, maintained and rebuilt the mechanical equipment used in that process, much of it old and in frequent need of restoration. He mended the fences and maintained the *acequias*, the bridge and the primitive roads. He and Arlene were totally responsible for the financial aspects of their modest but surprisingly complex small business, delivering their cattle to market, determining the timing of sales and purchasing the materials and supplies required by their enterprise. He didn't have the luxury of contracting out the other crafts such as plumbing, electrical and construction work that most of us ask others to do on our behalf. If something needed fixing, he taught himself how to fix it and he did the job himself.

In many ways it was a hard life and the financial rewards were modest, but the benefits were tangible. For the Garcias it was a satisfying life style and they had the pride of accomplishment that came from doing the whole job themselves. Most of us in our work lives, whether laborers, lawyers or corporate professionals perform only a small segment of a complex task. Even if our piece is challenging and complex we are only one player in an elaborate assembly line in which no one person can take credit for and enjoy the completion of the whole outcome.

Baudelio's work and his life are different in that he has the complex skills of an artisan who masters all of the talents required for the whole task. The piecemeal tasks that most of us perform in this complex global world deprive us of the satisfaction enjoyed by craftsmen of an earlier day. That is not to say that we would trade that satisfaction for the benefits of the twenty first century world such as longer lives, advanced medical care, leisure, economic security, life style options and the many other gifts of modern life, but the inherent rewards of our work life are often less palpable than they were in an earlier time.

Matt Crawford described this phenomenon in his book, *Shop Craft Is Soul Craft: An Inquiry into the Value of Work.* He said, "There is pride of accomplishment in the performance of whole tasks that can be held in the mind all at once, and contemplated as whole once finished." That thought captures the feeling that Baudelio expresses when he looks out over Santa Rita canyon and contemplates his life's work. And it translates into an appreciation of the beauty of the place where it all happened. He doesn't express it in extravagant terms but his love for the place is unmistakable and he does honor to that idea with a simple compliment. "It's pretty."

In the late spring of the next year, 1996, Chris and I were living and working in the project in a much more leisurely way, finishing things on the inside and out. As soon as the weather permitted in the following spring, Baudelio and I put on the exterior plaster color coat, shingled the eaves on the east and west ends of the house and started to shape the landscape around the house.

An almost finished handmade cabin.

As the intensity of the building process was winding down we had more time to look outward to the larger community of which we were a small part. Over the next fifteen years and more we came to know our *Hispano* neighbors better and learned much more about how they and many other families came to the place that they called Santa Rita. Most of them are now long gone from our little valley but their descendants are everywhere in the larger community of northern New Mexico and the San Luis Valley of Colorado and in many more distant places.

Afterword

There has been a lot of water under the bridge since 1995 and we should take stock of our cast of characters. When the Flints split off from our three party sharing of the old cabin, Forrest and Jean Smith gave some thought to doing the same thing. But on more mature reflection they decided to forego that adventure and they continued to share the cabin with Booker and Susan. Just a few years later, Forrest concluded that his health didn't allow him the full benefits of our shared property. He reluctantly decided that it was time for him to sell his interest to the other two families. It happened and the Kellys became the sole owners of the old cabin, reserving to the Smiths the right to occasional summer visits for several years. The Kellys and the Flints continued to jointly own the larger fifty acre tract that traced back to the Gallegos homestead.

When I first met Booker in 1956, he was already a veteran of open heart surgery, made necessary by damage done by rheumatic fever when he was young. He lived courageously with cardiac disease all his adult life and endured frequent surgeries. As he approached his seventies he found that he could no longer live full time at New Mexico's altitude. Faced with that problem he finally decided to retire from his law practice and he and Susan moved to the San Francisco Bay area where he could function more normally. Nonetheless they often returned for visits and maintained their passion for the old cabin and the valley. They began an extensive remodeling and expansion of the old place and Booker was able to enjoy several additional happy trips to supervise that project before his often repaired heart lost its final battle. Not long after his death, Susan returned to live full time in New Mexico and she and her children completed the improvements to the old place.

Forrest and Jean were occasional visitors in the valley, staying either in the "new" old place or in the Flint cabin. Jean had become a keen fly fisher and had many happy days on the stream. Forrest enjoyed several years of retirement from his own law practice before he fell ill with cancer and died. To the extent possible under the circumstances, Booker and Forrest are still with us in Santa Rita. Booker's ashes are under a wonderful monumental boulder in front of the old cabin. Forrest's ashes also came back to the valley but were more broadly disseminated. Jean, recalling that despite their friendship, Forrest and Booker didn't always see eye to eye, placed a portion of Forrest's ashes at a discrete distance from Booker's boulder, up the hill behind the cabin, probably on Forest Service property.

Another portion was distributed near the cabin of an upstream neighbor and friend who had been instrumental in introducing Booker and Forrest to what became our property back in 1977. The final vestige of Forrest's earthly remains was ceremoniously sprinkled by his family into the waters of the Rio de Los Pinos from the middle of our bridge across the river. As dyed in the wool New Mexicans we have all been glad to know that, like the water in the river, Forrest had little chance of ever reaching Texas. Jean reported that when the ashes hit the water, several trout broke the surface, as if rising to strike a May Fly; another Los Pinos legend in the making.

Another sad event affecting the human landscape of the valley was the death in 2012 of Baudelio's wife, Arlene. She, like Booker, died of chronic heart disease caused by childhood rheumatic fever. Then, tragically, just two months later, Baudelio's only son, a young man in his forties, died unexpectedly. Baudelio, with the support of his daughter Sandra and her husband, soldiers on in his lifelong work as a small scale interstate farmer and rancher with one foot in Colorado and the other in New Mexico. For that, all his friends in Santa Rita and beyond give our heartfelt thanks.

At the time of this writing, my family and I have shared this neighborhood with the Baudelio Garcia family and our outlander neighbors for longer than most of the original Santa Rita homesteaders persisted in this harsh but beautiful place. But that's because we are pampered, part time residents, enjoying all the benefits of twenty first century comfort and convenience. We have also learned that the gravitational pull of the home place, the *patria chica* as the old timers call it, is still strong among the families of those who lived here before we came. Many *Hispano* families now living in distant places still return regularly to visit the communities where their grandfathers lived and died. Many of the ancient and beautiful adobe churches throughout northern New Mexico have been restored and maintained by the people now dispersed across distant cities and states who return to lend their labor and resources to the effort. The beautiful little stone church in San Miguel, just down river from us, is an example of that tradition.

About ten years ago Chris and I were attending the funeral of Baudelio's sister Rose at the little cemetery down the road in the village of San Miguel. Among those attending the burial service was Elizaida Espinosa, the woman from whom we had bought our property in 1977. We had never met her face to face so it was a moving occasion for us. She was accompanied by her brother Gabriel Archuleta and two other siblings, all well into their eighties. Elizaida and her siblings had all left the valley not long after their father's death in 1931, she to Denver and her brothers to work in the mines of northern Colorado. But on that day they were all back in the valley for an old neighbor's funeral and to visit their family home and connect with childhood friends who were still in the larger San Luis valley neighborhood.

A summer or two later, Gabriel and his wife drove up to our cabin, unannounced, during another visit to the valley. We were delighted to welcome them. After a lively conversation on our porch, during which he told us stories about living in our old cabin as a child, he let us know that when he died he would like to be buried next to his father, Santiago Archuleta, in the family cemetery across the river on what was now our property. Of course we agreed. Two or three years later in the middle of another warm summer day, his family gathered at our place from California, Arizona and Colorado to bury his ashes in our little *camposanto*. The pull of the place was still strong.

Another more recent story shows the multi-generational connection of the unique New Mexico *Hispano* people to their home places. It relates to the old house right next door to our old cabin. It had been the home of Baudelio's parents, Juanita and Antonio Garcia when Baudelio and his six brothers and six sisters were children. Antonio, like most of the other early residents of Santa Rita, had been a farmer and rancher. He had also sometimes been an employee of the Denver and Rio Grande railroad that passed by just above his house. Baudelio recalls that his father received a small pension from the railroad in his later years. He thinks that the monthly check may have been only a few dollars.

All thirteen children lived to be adults and the parents lived well into their eighties, living in the old house full time until their last few years. Two of Baudelio's older brothers, Santiago and Octaviano, married and built their own houses nearby and lived in the canyon for a few years. One died tragically at a young age and the other remained in the valley, working for the railroad until he was struck down by cancer. Two other brothers, Manuel and Filemón went on to become school teachers. Both taught briefly in one room school houses in Santa Rita and down river in San Miguel. They later served in larger schools, Manuel in Conejos County, Colorado and Filemón in Tres Piedras, El Rito and Ojo Caliente in northern New Mexico. All of the girls in the family married and raised families in various San Luis Valley communities.

By the middle of the 1970s the senior Garcias had given up full time residency in Santa Rita and moved to modest but more comfortable quarters in Antonito, although they continued to spend summer periods in their canyon house. That left Baudelio and Arlene and their two children as the last *Hispano* family still living in Santa Rita and they too soon moved over the northern ridge to make their principal residence in Mogote, Colorado. But they continued to work the land and use their

Santa Rita house on a seasonal basis. The senior Garcias' house was no longer occupied and after their deaths it passed to their son, Manuel, who visited the old place occasionally but never occupied his parents' house. He even built two one room *casita*s on the property that he used as his living space on the few times that he overnighted in the canyon. He seemed to have almost a superstitious aversion to staying in the old house.

The decades passed and the old place gradually deteriorated and decayed, especially after Manuel's death, close to the end of the century. His children lived at a distance, some of them out of state, and had little interest in the property. But there was another Garcia waiting in the wings, one who had strong memories of his grandparents and the times he spent with them in their home when he was a small child. Chris Garcia is a son of Baudelio's brother Filemón. As a child he lived with his family in Santa Rita and later in San Miguel and several other communities where his father taught school. Chris went to college and then law school at the University of New Mexico in Albuquerque. After passing the state bar, he became a career attorney with the Legal Aid Office in Albuquerque.

While his work was in Albuquerque, Chris's heart remained in the north. His parents and siblings were in San Miguel, Antonito and the surrounding San Luis Valley. He owns property in the village of San Miguel and returns to the valley at every opportunity. When the heirs of

Manuel Garcia decided to give up the old house in Santa Rita, Chris bought the property and began to restore the old adobe house to what it had been when he visited his grandparents there in the 1960s. We met him there when he began that project in about 2009 and have shared stories with him as he became our neighbor and friend. His memories of growing up in the neighborhood and the stories he heard from his mother and father contributed importantly to my book about the settlement of the area and we continue our conversation about the place even today. He is learning more about his heritage and I am deepening my understanding of the history of our shared community.

In June of 2012 as I was finishing my history of the expansion of the *Hispano* homeland (*Hispano Homesteaders, The Last New Mexico Pioneers, 1850–1910*, also published by Sunstone Press), and the settlement of Santa Rita Canyon, I asked Chris to read my manuscript and share his reactions with me. What follows is part of our email correspondence that shows some of what we learned from each other about Santa Rita, its history and the larger story of the *Hispano* experience in northern New Mexico during the final period of settlement. The following is from a letter he wrote to me on the subject.

"I finished reading the manuscript this past Memorial Day weekend. I made it a point to read it while I was in San Miguel. It was extremely informative and I found it exciting to be able to know more about the homesteaders and subsequent residents, many of them being my relatives. I had a lot of different emotions and reactions that I will share with you."

In view of what follows, I should interject here that my working title for the book had been "Follow the Rivers North," since so much of the story of the northern expansion of the *Hispano* Homeland had been dictated by the availability of rivers and small streams that could support the agricultural and domestic needs of the settlers. My publisher recommended a title change to better attract reader interest. Chris's letter continues.

"First, I really liked the title. [Sorry Chris. So did I.] It made it sound like an adventure book which, to me, it really was. I was almost reliving the life of the homesteaders and those who followed. I could absolutely relate to your vivid description of the place, having lived in or being familiar with most of the area, even areas that had sort of been off limits to us for years. I had heard a lot of the names and stories from my father. I wish he was still around because your book would be four times as long. Unfortunately, he took a lot of history with him and that is our loss.

Your book tells us who homesteaded but it is still a mystery to me why they chose this area, especially considering how narrow the canyon becomes and how unsuitable for agriculture most of it is. I don't have any authority for it but I think a lot of it had to do with the fact that the homesteaders had access to the surrounding area for grazing their livestock and harvesting trees for lumber and firewood. Everyone seems to have raised sheep and they owned not only riding horses but also teams of horses for pulling their wagons, plows and even trees to build their bridges and houses. The depopulation of the area that you noted in the thirties was probably attributable in part to the creation of the national forest system. Up until that time the residents were able to use the forest with impunity. I think it was around this time that a strange new legal concept was introduced. The government started to limit the number of livestock that could be grazed in the national forest. Without unlimited access to what had now become the national forest, the residents' ability to earn a livelihood was severely impacted.

It was also at this time that the "tourists" began to discover the excellent fishing in the area. Many of them befriended the locals. They were known as the *güerros*. They were not called gringos but rather *güerros*, indicating the blond hair of the newcomers. These folks assisted the locals in selling their illegal products like homemade whiskey and later marijuana which could be sold in the outside world. As they became strapped for cash the locals also started selling their properties to the newcomers.

I also wonder what impact the railroad had on the depopulation of the canyon. I know that a number of the locals were working for the railroad. I do remember my dad saying that Osier and Sublette were thriving year round communities. The locals who worked there would walk or horseback ride back to their residences in the canyon on still existing trails from the nearby railroad towns. A lot of them eventually decided to move out of the canyon and down to the lower valley villages.

The depopulation you referred also had to do with the high infant mortality rate and an epidemic that killed many middle aged and elderly folks. [This is possibly a reference to the influenza epidemic of the teen years]. I know of at least 5 or 6 infants who if they had lived would have been my aunts and uncles. The local cemetery, like others in the area, is full of infant graves and of course there was usually not time to make and place a headstone or marker of any kind. I can just imagine what it took to bury someone in the middle of the winter. World Wars I and II were another contributing factor to the depopulation of the canyon. The men were drafted and many returned after the wars but none to the canyon. My grandmother Juanita and grandfather Antonio were the last and oldest people to live up in the canyon. Your manuscript does a very good job of describing the hard life these residents experienced. These folks were certainly survivors and able to sustain themselves. Unfortunately, as the youth grew up there was no hope for economic success in the canyon. Even though there was a school there, it was limited to the 8th grade. Thus if you wanted an education or a job you needed to move out and so it happened. I guess I could go on but for now I will call a time out. Hopefully we can connect this summer and continue this discussion."

Chris's thoughtful and informative letter gave me much to think about and of course our conversation continued. I agreed with him that it's hard to know why the early folks decided to go to such a hard place to make a living with such limited irrigation potential and I thought that what

Chris said made a lot of sense. That is, they didn't have many choices and the pioneers were not really farmers. They were herdsmen and ranchers. My research told me that as they moved north they built and maintained *acequias* but grew only a few crops. The small fields could only provide subsistence support for their families. They mainly grew crops to support their sheep and a few cattle for beef plus kitchen gardens to produce a few potatoes and vegetables during the short growing season. Their real livelihood was the animals that could be grazed in the forest in the warm months.

In earlier times in lower New Mexico, the *Hispano* people were given land grants under both Spanish and Mexican sovereignty. Families were granted small tracts called *suertes,* where they built their houses and irrigation facilities to grow crops for their own use. The community grants also provided large tracts of land called *ejidos* which were the common lands meant to be available to the whole community in perpetuity for grazing, timber and firewood harvesting, hunting and fishing. Unfortunately, under the American system of law and practice, most of these grants and especially the community rights were not protected. Chris was right to assume that when these people first came to Santa Rita, they were operating under the old ways of doing things. They had their own small tracts, acquired under the Homestead Act, usually less than one hundred acres, and expected to be able to use the forest as they always had under the Spanish and Mexican lgal systems.

Things changed under the American system. The national forests, created in the early 20th century, started imposing rules and regulations regarding grazing and, perhaps more damaging, started to impose fees for grazing permits. These subsistence ranchers had little access to cash and soon were under financial pressures they hadn't experienced before. Then another challenge came along in the form of property taxes. Even very low tax rates created big problems for people with no experience in the cash economy. My research showed that even in the early twentieth century many people had their properties sold for unpaid taxes of only a few dollars. Then they borrowed money from the mostly Anglo merchants and bankers which often led to forced sales to the newcomers.

Of course there were other factors at work. There was the attraction of opportunity in the new economy outside the rural communities. There were jobs in agriculture, local and state government, and the mines and then there were the wars and the opportunities to get into the majority culture by that avenue. There were some advantages to be gained by joining the majority culture and the more urban lifestyle. Chris's father and uncle were involved in that change as they became teachers and wage earners. Subsistence farming and ranching was a tough life and one not usually chosen if there were options. There must have been severe resentment among the people who went through these traumatic changes in life style and suffered the many forms of discrimination they experienced, especially when it involved being cut off from their traditional places, their *patrias chicas,* and the old way of life.

Our conversations with Chris Garcia, Baudelio Garcia and others continue even today and there is a strong thread in those conversations of the *Hispano* bond with the homeland. Coming home is a recurring theme in American literature, perhaps more so than in the literature of other cultures. Americans have always been a migratory people, first from other countries and continents and then from east to west in our own new country. For New Mexico *Hispanos*, the experience of coming home is qualitatively different than that of later immigrants to these shores, because when they come home, it is to a place and a cultural community where for three centuries they were the homogeneous majority. It had not been a way station on the Underground Railroad to integration and assimilation into the American mainstream. It was the final destination that they occupied exclusively as European immigrants, contested only by the Native Americans, who they gradually displaced.

The other hyphenated Americans don't have the same kind of home to return to, a home place that has a persistent ethnic character. There were the little Italies, German towns, China towns, Japan towns and the countless other ethnic enclaves for Hungarians, Poles, Serbs and the dozens of other nationalities that came this way. Many of these cultural islands were in urban places while others were rural and Midwestern including communities dominated, among many others, by Norwegians, Swedes, Danes, Swiss and Germans. And as the immigrants were transient, their original American cultural home places slowly faded away too, especially in the cities. So even if descendants of the original wanderers wanted to return to their original places in America, the places themselves usually no longer existed as culturally distinct communities. And many of those who stayed behind and didn't follow the westward migration, became fully integrated members of the majority American mainstream with less identification to their cultural roots.

The case of the northern New Mexico *Hispano* is truly unique. When they stayed in their traditional homeland, as many did, or when they later came home again, as many did, it was to a place they had occupied uncontested by other European immigrants for hundreds of years. They were and continue to be the first new Americans in this vast region. And their sense of that status is still strong in Northern New Mexico. When we stop for lunch at the Mesa Vista Café in Ojo Caliente, we always get a warm reception, not to mention a great red chile cheese enchilada with onions and *refritos*. The restaurant has been operated for two generations by the Chacon family. Often the men at the next table are having an animated conversation in northern New Mexico Spanish, conscious of but unconcerned with the fact that we Anglos can't be a part of that conversation. They are comfortable knowing that they are speaking their own language in their own country and that as long as they are able to do so and stay in their place, Spanish will be the lingua franca and their small communities in Rio Arriba and Taos Counties will be their *patrias chicas*, their homeland. And no matter how many of us come here to live, it is their place and we are visitors or at best the new neighbors. That strikes me as being a wonderful relationship. I applaud their resilience and persistence in the face of overwhelming odds. They are still here. The newcomers have often taken over their land grants. Many of their old ranches are now gated enclaves. Their *acequias* and water rights are at risk. But, in the Mesa Vista Café, they are still the ones who can call this home.

It is compelling to consider the divergent paths taken by our family and by Chris Garcia that ultimately brought us to share this place. We moved in and built a second home for ourselves in Santa Rita, a remnant community at the northern edge of the *Hispano* Homeland. Chris began his life here but moved out to achieve an education, a profession and employment in the outside world. And then as we continued to settle in he was drawn back to recover and restore the home of his grandparents. We built a new house in an old place. He is rescuing an old house that contains the memories of his childhood and the imprint of his forebears. We came to our two endeavors from opposite directions but with common purpose; to respect, preserve and love a place we appreciate for its beauty and the pleasure it gives us but also to value it for what had been here before we arrived. And it can't be forgotten that an important link in our chain of connection was the role played in our lives by Chris's uncle and our neighbor and friend, Baudelio Garcia.

Harlan Flint and Baudelio Garcia—Straw Bale Partners.

CPSIA information can be obtained
at www.ICGtesting.com
Printed in the USA
LVHW060507310821
696471LV00008B/830